The MINNESOTA BOOK of SKILLS

The MINNESOTA BOOK of SKILLS

Your Guide to Smoking Whitefish,
Sauna Etiquette, Tick Extraction, and More

Chris Niskanen

MINNESOTA HISTORICAL SOCIETY PRESS

www.mhspress.org

The Minnesota Historical Society Press is a member of the Association of American University Presses.

Manufactured in the United States of America

10 9 8 7 6 5 4 3 2

∞ The paper used in this publication meets the minimum requirements of the American National Standard for Information Sciences—Permanence for Printed Library Materials, ANSI Z39.48–1984.

International Standard Book Number
ISBN: 978-0-87351-868-0 (cloth)
ISBN: 978-0-87351-884-0 (e-book)

Library of Congress Cataloging-in-Publication Data
Niskanen, Chris.
    The Minnesota book of skills : your guide to smoking whitefish, sauna etiquette, tick extraction, and more / Chris Niskanen.
        p. cm.
    Includes bibliographical references and index.
    ISBN 978-0-87351-868-0 (cloth. : alk. paper) — ISBN 978-0-87351-884-0 (e-book)
1. Survival skills—Minnesota. 2. Minnesota—Social life and customs. 3. Minnesota—Life skills guides. I. Title.
    GF86.N57 2012
    646.709776—dc23
    2012022471

Contents

For my mother, whose skills always inspire

Introduction

FOR TWENTY-THREE YEARS I worked as a newspaper outdoors writer with an aversion to a genre known as the "how-to" story. To be sure, there were times when I offered advice on the best shotgun pellets for hunting pheasants or bait for catching walleyes (leeches or minnows?), but since this knowledge is readily available in the hook and bullet magazines, I thought, why repeat it unnecessarily in a newspaper column?

Besides, there was better fodder in the fascinating people and places I encountered across on my beat. My job was to tell their stories. Or so my readers told me.

Then one autumn I came across a story about a family who had spent an entire year preparing for Thanksgiving dinner. They decided to make the holiday feast more interesting by not using a single store-bought ingredient except salt. (For a sugar substitute, they figured they could tap maple and box elder trees for sweet syrup, but a similar source for raw salt isn't readily available in Minnesota.)

This was a clan of organic dairy farmers, hunters, anglers, gardeners, foragers, and beekeepers. They had the skills to pull off this one-of-a-kind meal. But more importantly, they thought it would be great family fun to create this special dinner. My readers agreed. The story ran on the front page of the *St. Paul Pioneer Press*, and it was the most popular story on the newspaper's website that Thanksgiving Day.

The story got me thinking about self-sufficient skills—the ones practiced by my grandparents and parents—and the ones that are unique to living in Minnesota.

I come from a long line of German and Scandinavian farmers and small-business owners whose skills got them through hard times. My mother, who lived in a log cabin until she was eleven, recalls eating venison for most of her childhood because deer were essentially free, but beef wasn't.

My grandmothers picked wild berries and made them into syrups, sauces, and puddings because store-bought fruit in northern Minnesota was expensive. Like many women of their generation, they knew how to sew their own clothes, milk a cow, preserve food, and cook for large families. My grandfathers could overhaul engines, raise a herd of cattle, shoot a deer rifle, and tell a good story. My father never farmed, but he could do all those other things, too.

About the same time I wrote the Thanksgiving story, my mother-in-law gave me a copy of *The Foxfire Book*, a 1972 best seller about Appalachian folk culture and skills. The book began as a series of magazine articles written in the 1960s by high school students at Rabun Gap–Nacoochee School in Georgia, at the south end of the Appalachians. While the articles started as a writing assignment, the *Foxfire* books established a new style of "learner-centered" education, where students make decisions about how they learn and use local residents as resources. They interviewed their subjects and reported on how to make moonshine, dress a hog, and plant crops by astrological signs. The folk-skills books appealed to a whole generation of Americans eager to live closer to the land.

The book piqued my interest in skills. What are those skills we practice in the much colder climate here in Minnesota? Drawing from my own familial experience, I started making a list and quickly reached a hundred skills. Some were modern, some were a few generations old, and some have been around since Native Americans were the only inhabitants of North America. And some are uniquely part of Minnesota culture.

As I researched *The Minnesota Book of Skills*, I began to find people who were as interesting as the skills they possessed. I met Alan Burchell, a septuagenarian who still takes his boat out on bitterly cold November evenings to net whitefish from Lake Kabetogama. Our conversations about how he broils and smokes these delectable white-meat fish made my mouth water. Then there was Erik Simula, who keeps alive the dying art of building birch-bark canoes in northern Minnesota and who once paddled one of his canoes a thousand miles in a summer.

A friend told me about crop artist Liz Schreiber, who strolls the aisles of her local food co-op in search of seeds to create her prizing-winning art. I learned that one of the nation's finest waterfowl painters, Joe Hautman, has a PhD in physics. Francois Fouquerel, dean of the French Voyageur program at the Concordia Language Village in Moorhead, has spent a good part of his career teaching schoolchildren how to sing like voyageurs. He spends summers singing voyageur songs during canoe trips along the same routes traveled by voyageurs.

What is it that draws people to hone these skills that are seemingly less important in our high-tech society?

Greg Wright, the executive director of the North House Folk School, thinks he knows the answer. His school in Grand Marais aspires to be the counterpoint to our high-tech, low-touch world. North House students come from across the country to learn Old World skills, but they mostly come to use their hands in ways that don't involve a computer keyboard.

"Our hands are not connected to the joy and necessity of creating the things of our lives," Greg says. "That's not necessarily a bad thing. Without question, extracting your life from the landscape around you is very hard work, but in the convenience of the day, we've lost something. The idea that we can grab a resource around us and use it to help sustain our life—that's profound."

My list of important Minnesota skills doesn't always reach for the profound. Extracting a biting deer tick is the kind of know-how that makes sense—no one wants any of the nasty diseases these buggers carry. Ditto for removing ice dams, which I've done with some frequency, climbing a ladder to break away a glacial-like formation in my gutters, but I never quite understood the mechanics of ice dams until I did some research.

But one of the reasons we strive to learn new skills is to make connections with each other. Some skill is required to build your own backyard ice rink, but one of the results is your neighbors showing up with their ice skates to take a few turns on your sheet of ice. Who knew the neighborhood would appreciate your efforts to fill the evening air with the sound of kids shooting pucks? Or so Brian and Gretchen Gunderson discovered when they built their Stillwater ice rink.

While you can learn to do anything from the Internet, people still want to share their ideas in person. They want to learn from each other, swap notes, and admire each other's work. Carving a wooden bowl from instructions found online isn't the same as learning it in person from a craftsman, says Greg, whose school offers a wide selection of woodcraft classes. "People leave our school with their wooden bowl, but they leave laughing, hugging, and enchanted with the humanity of it," he says.

I started *The Minnesota Book of Skills* thinking I was writing a how-to book, but when I was done, I realized it was really about the fascinating people and places behind those skills, and that I'd come full circle once again.

The MINNESOTA BOOK of SKILLS

Bread baking demonstration, 1925

Grow Your Own Wheat

FLOUR IS EASY TO TAKE FOR GRANTED. It comes from the store in large, sturdy bags and it is relatively inexpensive. But what about growing your own wheat and making flour? In the 1800s, Minneapolis was known as the Flour Milling Capital of the World, and the state still ranks among the top states in wheat production, but some gardeners today are going even more local and growing the grain in their backyards.

Florence and Dave Minar own an organic dairy, Cedar Summit, near New Prague. They and their children are a family of do-it-yourselfers, home bakers, and gardeners. With their skills and love of family projects, they were inspired to start a Thanksgiving tradition where everyone attending would bring a homemade dish. They went one step further by requiring every family member to use homegrown ingredients, including the flour. It was a novel challenge to see how self-reliant they could be on a holiday that honors self-reliance.

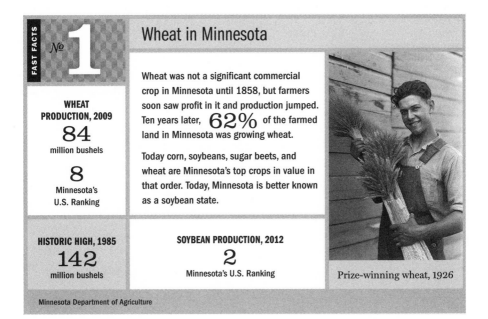

FAST FACTS

№ **1**

Wheat in Minnesota

Wheat was not a significant commercial crop in Minnesota until 1858, but farmers soon saw profit in it and production jumped. Ten years later, **62%** of the farmed land in Minnesota was growing wheat.

Today corn, soybeans, sugar beets, and wheat are Minnesota's top crops in value in that order. Today, Minnesota is better known as a soybean state.

WHEAT PRODUCTION, 2009
84
million bushels

8
Minnesota's
U.S. Ranking

HISTORIC HIGH, 1985
142
million bushels

SOYBEAN PRODUCTION, 2012
2
Minnesota's U.S. Ranking

Prize-winning wheat, 1926

Minnesota Department of Agriculture

3

A lifelong dairy and grain farmer, Dave Minar knew how to raise wheat but hadn't grown it for decades. For this project, he knew he didn't want to plant a whole field. He needed just enough for pastries and bread for the Thanksgiving meal. Still, this part of the meal would take some planning.

Wheat is actually not difficult to grow. In fact, the local food movement has spurred a number of organic gardening magazines, like *Mother Earth News*, to publish articles on backyard wheat production. Because Minnesota still ranks in the top ten nationally in wheat production, finding wheat seed here isn't a problem.

"I was able to get organic spring wheat from a dealer in Gaylord," Dave says. "I decided on growing a plot that was twenty by thirty feet. The yield was very good. I'm guessing about thirty-five bushels to the acre."

There are two types of wheat: spring and winter. Farmers plant winter wheat in the fall and harvest it in midsummer. Spring wheat is planted in the spring, typically around May in Minnesota, and harvested in early fall. Dave harvested his spring wheat at the end of August, after the stalks turned from green to yellow and brown and the heads were heavy with grain.

How do you cut wheat? In the old days, farmers used scythes and later primitive cutting and threshing machines. Dave's plot was too small to require mechanic cutting. "I just hand harvested the wheat by cutting off the heads with a knife and putting them in a tub," he says.

Threshing—separating the straw and chaff from the wheat—was next. One simple method still practiced around the world is to flail the wheat with a wooden stick. Grain flails are typically two sticks—a long one for the handle and a shorter one for the flail—that are connected by a piece of leather. The technique can be tricky to keep from hitting yourself with the short stick, but the idea is to whack the grain repeatedly to break the wheat heads apart.

"I couldn't persuade [my wife] Florence to wear a floor-length dress and hand flail the heads like the ladies did a century and a half ago," Dave says, "so I came up with an easier system using a baseball bat." When his wheat was dry and ready to thresh, he drove the top of the bat into the wheat to separate it from the head. All this was done in a tub.

From there "we used a fan or the wind, if it was windy, to glean the chaff from the seed," Dave says. This process, also known as winnowing, uses air movement to blow the chaff away from the wheat kernels. It is done by pouring the wheat from one container to another.

The next problem was grinding the wheat into flour. Back in the 1970s, when her children were growing up, Florence ground her own flour from wheat kernels using an electric flour mill. She and Dave were able to find the old mill in their barn, and they set to work grinding their wheat.

As Thanksgiving approached, Florence faced another dilemma. The meal's rules didn't allow store-bought yeast or baking soda, and her attempts to start a sourdough didn't work out as she had hoped. So instead of bread, she decided to make yeast-free popovers for Thanksgiving. The popovers were delicious and the perfect complement to the roast venison and wild turkey, homegrown vegetables, and other dishes the family made from scratch.

Tick Identification and Extraction

Ticks are nasty. Anyone who has been bitten by one—an awful experience itself—has had that dreadful, lingering question of whether some disease was injected into their veins. The words "Lyme disease" have gone mainstream in the outdoors lexicon, but the creepy parasites also carry other diseases such as human anaplasmosis and babesiosis that can make you seriously ill. I have not had any of these diseases, but I have friends who have Lyme and anaplasmosis. One outdoorsman I know was treated for three separate tick-borne diseases from a single bite.

According to the Minnesota Department of Health, the culprit in all this nastiness is the blacklegged tick, also known as the deer tick. The blacklegged is much smaller than the wood or dog tick, and the blacklegged females and nymphs are the ones that transmit diseases through their bite. The female—larger than males, nymphs, and larvae—is about one-eighth of an inch long and can be difficult to identify. The female is red and dark brown, and the males, nymphs, and larvae are tiny and dark.

So unless you're an entomologist with a magnifying glass, you're unlikely to make a clear ID of a blacklegged tick from a small wood tick. Besides, most people in a panicky situation squish the little buggers beyond recognition.

These tips from the Minnesota Department of Natural Resources are designed to avoid all ticks, disease carriers and not:

» When you're in tick-infested areas, use a repellent containing DEET or permethrin and follow the application directions on the container.

» Tuck your pants into your socks or boots and your long-sleeved shirt into your pants to create a barrier to ticks trying to reach your skin.

» Wear light-colored clothing so clinging ticks are more visible.

» When you come inside from tick territory, remove your clothes, check your body for ticks, shower, and towel off vigorously. Check your clothes for ticks and wash them right away.

» Check your pets frequently for ticks.

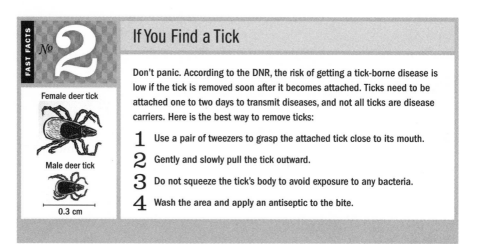

FAST FACTS № 2

If You Find a Tick

Don't panic. According to the DNR, the risk of getting a tick-borne disease is low if the tick is removed soon after it becomes attached. Ticks need to be attached one to two days to transmit diseases, and not all ticks are disease carriers. Here is the best way to remove ticks:

1 Use a pair of tweezers to grasp the attached tick close to its mouth.

2 Gently and slowly pull the tick outward.

3 Do not squeeze the tick's body to avoid exposure to any bacteria.

4 Wash the area and apply an antiseptic to the bite.

Female deer tick

Male deer tick

0.3 cm

Lyme Disease Symptoms

According to the Mayo Clinic, a small red bump may appear on the site of the tick bite, and over the next few days the redness may expand and form a rash in a bull's-eye pattern.

There are other symptoms to watch out for:

» Feels like the flu. You may feel chills, fatigue, fever, body aches.

» If left untreated, the infection may cause you to feel bouts of joint pain and swelling several weeks to months after you're infected.

» More serious symptoms may include swelling around the brain, paralysis of one side of your face, and numbness or weakness in your limbs.

According to the Mayo Clinic, the standard treatment for early-stage Lyme disease is oral antibiotics such as doxycycline or amoxicillin. Advanced cases may involve intravenous antibiotic treatments.

How to Harvest Wild Rice

WILD RICE, or *manoomin* in the Ojibwe language, is not rice, but a variety of grass that is both delicious and higher in protein than most grains. In addition to being a sacred crop to the Ojibwe, wild rice has been a cash grain in northern Minnesota for years, though naturally growing rice has been largely replaced in grocery stores by cultivated wild rice.

The good news is that naturally growing wild rice is still abundant in central and northern Minnesota and available for the taking, as long as you have the right equipment, a license, and a strong back.

Where to Find Wild Rice

Wild rice grows in seven hundred lakes throughout thirty-one counties in Minnesota, but the bulk of lakes supporting natural rice are in Aitkin, Cass, Crow Wing, Itasca, and St. Louis counties. Wild rice grows best in water that is six inches to three feet deep and in flowages with slowly moving water. It is an annual plant that grows from seeds dropped the previous year. While hundreds of lakes have rice, finding an adequate and accessible bed for harvesting takes skill and experience, and veteran wild ricers aren't likely to share their secret spots with you.

If you want to try your hand at wild ricing and you don't know a veteran ricer to take you out, visit the Department of Natural Resources website (www.mndnr.gov) and read about wild rice lakes regulated and managed by the agency and Ojibwe bands around the state. The agency has lots of information about wild ricing, wild rice lakes, and regulations and is interested in promoting rice harvesting, which is increasingly becoming a dying art. The number of wild rice licenses sold by the DNR has dropped from a high of sixteen thousand in 1968 to fewer than fifteen hundred in recent years.

When to Harvest Wild Rice

The wild rice season runs from August 15 to September 30, from 9 AM to 3 PM daily, but the precise time when individual stands mature depends on weather and water levels. It is illegal to harvest unripened "green" rice. Harvest dates are often set on individual lakes and announced by the DNR after local inspections. Rice is ready to be harvested when it easily falls off the plant. In general, you can count on wild rice to be ripe somewhere in the state around Labor Day weekend.

FAST FACTS

№ **3**

How to Cook Wild Rice

1 cup wild rice

3 cups water or chicken broth

1 teaspoon salt

(skip salt if you're using commercial chicken broth, which typically already is salted)

Rinse rice. Place in saucepan with water or broth and salt. Bring to a boil and simmer for 45 to 50 minutes. Check for tenderness; drain excess liquid. For chewier texture, reduce cooking time. Makes about 2 to 3 cups.

Grace Rogers and Joe Aitken harvesting wild rice near Walker, 1939

Who Can Harvest

Residents and nonresidents can buy licenses to harvest wild rice. A seasonal resident license is twenty-five dollars; a one-day license is fifteen dollars. For nonresidents, the only option is a one-day license for thirty dollars. Licenses can be purchased from DNR license outlets. About three to five thousand people are estimated to harvest wild rice annually.

Equipment

You'll need a canoe that doesn't exceed eighteen feet long and thirty-six inches wide, according to state law.

You'll also need a push pole, available at many marine supply stores. A push pole is fifteen feet or longer with an aluminum "duckbill," which springs open when placed against the lake bottom so your pole doesn't disappear into the mud.

Flails, or knockers, are a pair of smooth round sticks that are used to pull wild stalks over the canoe's gunwales and to knock the rice off the plants. By law, flails can't be longer than thirty inches and weigh more than a pound. It's good to have a few grain bags, such as those used at feed mills, to store and transport your rice.

How It's Done

Here's where a strong back is needed. The canoe is pushed through the rice beds with the push pole while the "knocker" sits in the canoe and uses the flails to harvest the rice. The knocker gently bends the plants into the canoe with one stick and taps or strokes the rice off the stalk with the other. Depending on the abundance of rice in the bed, you could harvest a few pounds to several hundred pounds in a single day.

Getting It Processed

Once you have harvested the wild rice, it still needs to go through the parching, hulling, and cleaning stages before it's ready to be cooked. Some veteran wild ricers parch their own rice, but most wild rice harvesters bring their grain to a professional processor. Processors are becoming a rarity these days—the art of processing naturally grown and harvested wild rice is disappearing, along with the tradition of wild ricing—but the DNR maintains a list of processors and their contact information on its website. Check there for a wild rice processor near you.

Whitefish Netting and Smoking

WHITEFISH NETTING is a disappearing method of capturing one of Minnesota's tastiest fish. Alan Burchell remembers netters flocking to Lake Kabetogama in the 1950s and '60s to brave the rough and cold waters in late fall when the fish converge on shallow reefs to spawn.

"You'd set your net at night and go duck hunting the next morning," says Alan, seventy, a former resort owner who still lives on the lake. "People would drive over from the Iron Range just to catch some whitefish. It's an old tradition that has died off."

Minnesota has whitefish populations in Lake Superior and in a number of deep, cold inland lakes. A handful of commercial anglers still net whitefish in Lake Superior and sell fresh and smoked whitefish and whitefish roe, which is marketed as caviar. It is the inland netting tradition that has faded, perhaps because of the weather extremes netters must endure in late October and early November. Also, the popular seasons of duck hunting and deer hunting occur during the same period, attracting about a half million hunters annually.

Alan helps to keep the tradition alive. His father netted fish on Kabetogama, but it wasn't until 1983 that Alan began to learn the habits of whitefish and how to net them. He's netted about twenty-one hundred whitefish during the past thirty years, giving most of them away to grateful friends and neighbors and canning, smoking, or baking the rest.

How to Net Whitefish

On Lake Kabetogama, spawning whitefish stage on rocky reefs to spawn between mid-October and mid-November. Alan says the "prime time" to net them is October 24 to November 12 when the water temperatures lower to between forty-five and forty-one degrees. "They usually run for about two to two and a half weeks."

A special whitefish netting license is required from the Department of Natural Resources, and a netter is allowed to set only one net. Alan prefers a one-hundred-foot-long monofilament net with a two-and-a-half-inch mesh.

Using a boat, Alan sets the nets in the evening on shallow, offshore reefs. The reefs are no deeper than six feet, and the ideal depth to set the net is four feet. The whitefish school on the reefs at night to spawn in the rubble and gravel, which will hold their eggs until spring incubation. Because there are so many whitefish and so few netters, capturing the fish on their spawning grounds doesn't affect their populations.

Alan checks the net the next morning. He averages about five fish per net lift. A good catch is a dozen fish. Spawning whitefish can weigh between four and ten pounds, so a lift of five or six fish over five pounds each can be quite a heavy haul.

Whitefish: A Delicacy

Alan butterflies his whitefish by cutting the fish along the backbone and keeping the belly intact. He cuts off the head and tail and then brines the fish in a saltwater solution to tenderize and flavor it for smoking and baking. A favorite is broiling the fillets with a special sauce made by his wife, Miriam.

"The meat is richer than walleye," he says. Whitefish also yield more meat than other fish: "A standard boneless walleye fillet is about 40 percent of gross weight and

Alan Burchell hauls in the last net of the season

a northern pike is closer to 50 percent. But because of its small head and body structure, a whitefish fillet is about 60 percent gross weight."

Smoking Whitefish

To smoke whitefish, Alan starts by cleaning the fish the same as he would for baking it: by removing head, guts, tail fin, and scales, splitting it down the back, removing the pin bone strip from the cut side, and leaving the belly meat intact. He brines the fillet in salt water, which gives the fish flavor and tenderizes it. To test for proper salinity in the brine, he mixes in enough salt to float an egg. He soaks the whitefish fillets for about half a day (less for smaller fish), then rinses and dries the fillets. He prepares several each time, wrapping and freezing many for later use.

He uses a wood-fired smoker and maple as his smoke agent, although he also recommends fruit or nut trees (but not mesquite because the imparted flavor is too strong for the fish). He places the brined fillet skin side–down on a wire rack in a shallow pan covered with a porous weave cloth to catch excess tar. He puts some water in the bottom of the pan, places the pan in the smoker, and smokes the fillet for around four hours. "Remove the fillet when the flesh is white and still juicy," he says. While there is nothing tastier than a warm, smoked whitefish fresh out of the smoker, Alan's work isn't done there. He and Miriam pressure cook and puree the leftover bones lifted from the meat to create tasty fish broth, used later for vegetable soup.

FAST FACTS   № 4

Miriam's Heavenly Fish Sauce for Baked Whitefish

2 pounds whitefish fillets	3 tablespoons mayonnaise
2 tablespoons lemon juice	3 tablespoons chopped green onion
½ cup grated Parmesan cheese	¼ teaspoon salt
¼ cup butter, softened	dash hot pepper sauce

Place whitefish fillets in a single layer on a well-greased bake-and-serve platter. Brush fillets with lemon juice and let stand 10 minutes. To make the sauce, combine remaining ingredients, blend well, and place in serving bowl. Broil fillets about 4 inches from source of heat for 6 to 8 minutes and serve with sauce.

Smoking whitefish

Build Your Own Backyard Ice Rink

BRIAN GUNDERSON played high school hockey in Stillwater. Now that he and his wife, Gretchen, have three rambunctious boys of their own, it was natural that the Gundersons began thinking about building a backyard rink.

Once Brian began asking around about how to build backyard rinks and looking for information on the Internet, he realized there is a burgeoning industry of do-it-yourself rink-builders. "There might be hundreds of rinks in Stillwater," he says. "There were already a couple in my neighborhood, and it wasn't long before I was getting advice from other hockey dads."

Brian built his first rink in his side yard, between the driveway and the neighbor's fence. He learned enough from the first winter to make improvements and create a new rink every winter.

The Gundersons' boys, Isaac, Aidan, and Sam, are ages twelve, ten, and six, respectively. They spend their spare time shooting pucks into their goalie nets and playing hockey with their buddies.

Their rink is also a beehive of neighborhood activity. A neighbor bought his wife ice skates for Christmas and taught her to skate at the Gundersons' backyard rink. Others drop by to skate or shoot pucks. The neighbors say how much they like to hear the sounds of kids playing in the evening, the *swoosh* of skates and the *tink* of pucks against the goal pipes. "I love the social aspect of the rink," Gretchen says. "We have adult neighbors who come over and skate at night and kids who learn to skate on our rink. It's a gathering place for families in our neighborhood."

Backyard Rink Basics

Ideally, says Brian, you start your backyard rink with a flat surface. With a level yard, you can erect sideboards and flood the area with a garden hose, first by soaking the ground and creating the first sheet of ice and then continually building on top of that.

But the Gundersons' yard isn't flat, so Brian began to search for a rink liner that would hold water and create a level surface where his yard isn't level. An Internet search yielded companies that sell liners designed specifically for backyard ice rinks. He bought one for about three hundred dollars. His rink is twenty-five feet by fifty feet, and the rule of thumb is the liner should be five feet wider both in width and length so it can fold over the sideboards.

Brian says his first liner lasted two seasons, after which he purchased another one from a farm supply store. This time, it was a silo liner that farmers use to keep moisture out of their grain storage bins. He cut the liner in two and shared it with a friend who also has a backyard rink. By splitting the cost with his friend, the silo liner ended up costing Brian about one hundred dollars.

Sideboards keep the liner vertical and the water and ice inside the rink. Brian uses two-by-ten pine boards for his sideboards and connects them with scraps of lumber and deck screws. He strategically places fence posts around the outside of the boards to give them vertical strength; the posts are wrapped with soft, protective foam insulation. Commercially made sideboards can be purchased—they're typically made of strong plastic—and some backyard rink enthusiasts have picked up sideboards from community or city rinks that are replacing them or getting out of the rink business due to budget cuts.

Brian's sideboards rise four courses high (meaning his two-by-ten boards are stacked on edge four high), but his sons want him to make the boards higher so their pucks don't fly out of the rink into the yard. "Netting around the rink is one of the things I'm going to invest in soon," he says.

Filling It Up

Usually starting after Thanksgiving, Brian begins closely monitoring the weather and below-freezing temperatures so he can fill up his rink. The ideal conditions for filling a rink are cold days and no snow. "I'm constantly watching the weather," Brian says.

"Sometimes he's up until two o'clock in the morning," says Gretchen.

"It's quiet and peaceful in the neighborhood that time of night," Brian replies.

Under good conditions, he can fill up his rink in about four nights. He doesn't know how many gallons it takes, but he guesses "it's in the thousands." He recalls the winter of 2010–11 was ideal for filling his rink because there was a long stretch of cold weather that allowed him to lay down a solid layer of ice. The following winter was disastrous. The mild winter was never consistently cold to keep the rink in good shape, Brian says.

But once it was cold enough to start making rinks, his network of ice-making dads were constantly in contact, exchanging tips and laments. "We're always getting together and comparing notes," he says.

Maintaining a Perfect Sheet

Brian uses a small snowblower and several snow shovels to keep his rink clear of snow. He also built his own handheld Zamboni of sorts. The contraption is made of galvanized pipe with a hose connect at one end. It is shaped like a T, and the top of the T has a series of holes drilled into it. The length of the T is the handle, with the hose connection in the end. Connected to the hose, the instrument allows water to flow through the holes and soak a cotton bath mat that wraps around the end of the pipe (imagine it as a large, T-shaped mop with the bath mat oozing water). Brian pushes his handheld Zamboni back and forth across the ice, laying down a thin water layer that turns to ice. He said the design can be found easily online.

Brian uses the device to add an extra layer of ice after the boys have scraped up the surface with their skates. "It fills in all the cracks and nicks nicely and lays down a nice layer of ice," he says.

After the Season

When the weather warms and the skating season ends, Brian opens one corner of the rink and allows the water to drain away into the street gutter. Once the ice disappears, he folds up the liner and disassembles the sideboards for storage. His rink doesn't kill his grass, which returns every summer despite the winter use. Brian says he's noticed fewer weeds in his grass every spring since he's been erecting his rink. "Maybe the rink kills the weeds or doesn't allow them to get into the grass," he says.

Storage is a big issue for backyard rinks. Brian says he is lucky his father has a large pole barn where the parts of the rink are stored during the off-season.

Sauna Etiquette

AN INVITATION TO VISIT A SAUNA usually begs a nervous question from the novice sauna user: clothes or no clothes? In Finland and among Finnish Americans, the sauna's purpose is to cleanse the body and soul, so wearing clothes in the steam

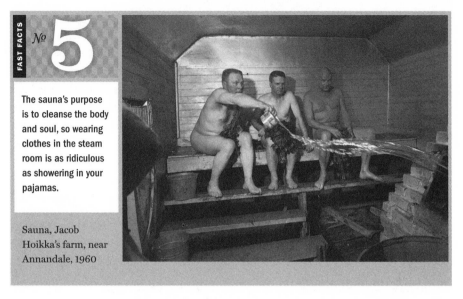

№ 5

The sauna's purpose is to cleanse the body and soul, so wearing clothes in the steam room is as ridiculous as showering in your pajamas.

Sauna, Jacob Hoikka's farm, near Annandale, 1960

room is as ridiculous as showering in your pajamas. But novices are usually cut a little slack and may be allowed to wear a swimsuit. However, they soon learn it's not comfortable sitting in 160-degree heat with any clothes on, even a swimsuit.

In traditional Finnish sauna culture, one behaves inside a sauna as one would inside a church. No loud talking, swearing, or drinking alcohol. (Besides, beer quickly gets warm in a well-heated sauna, so it's best to keep it outside in the snow.) The sauna experience should be free of distractions (cell phones) and metal objects that will conduct heat and become very hot (jewelry, wristwatches). Discussing a person's weight loss or gain is generally discouraged because no one really cares what you look like, and it only draws attention to your naked body. You're in a sauna for relaxation and friendship, and nothing distracts more from that than self-analysis.

Be sure to bring a water bottle and your good humor into the sauna. A sauna will naturally bring out your storytelling gene, so be prepared to reminisce about high school, an embarrassing moment abroad, or the time you fell in love on the Ferris wheel at the state fair. You can also sit quietly and enjoy the smell of the steam and wood and perhaps a hint of wood smoke, a combination that Finns affectionately call *löyly*.

Afterward, you may be invited to jump into a frozen lake or roll in the snow, which isn't as bad as it sounds.

DIY Death Rituals

THE NOTIONS OF "GREEN" BURIALS and do-it-yourself funeral arrangements are gaining ground as more Americans weigh the cost of burials and question the need for expensive metal caskets.

The trend has surfaced as a class offered by the North House Folk School in Grand Marais. The three-day class, called "Bury Yourself in Your Work: Build Your Own Casket," is taught by Randy Schnobrich, who moved from Wisconsin to the woods north of Grand Marais seventeen years ago to enjoy a simpler life and a career as a woodworker and carpenter.

The class was started in the late 1980s by well-known North House boatbuilder Mark Hanson. It typically attracts three to four students for each class. Schnobrich has taught the class four times. He says some people take the class intending to use the casket in the near future; others aren't planning to die soon but build the simple pine box for a relative or for a unique woodworking experience.

"About a fourth of the class is people interested in woodworking, and many people take it because it's a peculiar woodworking class and a good way to learn skills," Schnobrich says. "At least half of them sincerely want the casket for themselves. It is really important for them to have an attachment to their casket. They want to personalize it. For others, it's monetary and the idea of a green burial."

Schnobrich says he doesn't intentionally veer into philosophical or spiritual subjects during the woodworking class, but the act of constructing a casket can become a powerful experience. One of his students was a woman battling cancer; she insisted on taking the class despite the toll chemo treatments were taking on her body. Schnobrich says the woman approached the class and her impending death with humor and strength. "I probably teared up more than she did," he says, recalling that the woman died several months after the class and fulfilled her wish to be buried in her personal casket.

Many of the students have minimal woodworking skills but a zest for the unique project. One woman milled the wood from a dead pecan tree in her parents' yard and used the boards to make caskets for them. The school allows students to bring a partner to help work on one casket, and couples sometimes take the course together.

While most of the students come from Minnesota, others have come from as far away as California, Maine, and New York.

"I think there is a greater appreciation today for the natural world and green living, and more people are making death a part of that," Schnobrich says. "You can spend $15,000 for a funeral or $1,500. There is absolutely a trend toward a simpler life."

Tuition for the class is $225 and the materials cost $475, which is far cheaper than the thousands that modern coffins can cost.

Constructing the Coffin

The North House Folk School sticks to the principle of simplicity in a coffin: a box made with cabinet-grade pine, with four sides and a lid. Schnobrich mills some of the wood materials himself but purchases most of the lumber from a local lumberyard and preps the one-inch-thick boards before the class. He will glue together boards for rough lengths and widths. Before the class, he asks each student whether the coffin is for them or someone else, which figures into the final dimensions of the box.

During class, students cut the boards to specific lengths, sand them by hand, and cut the joints that attach the boards at each corner. "In the spirit of the school, we try not to machine a lot of the project," Schnobrich explains. "We try to get by with hand tools and a couple of hand planers." That also means using hand sanders, not powered orbital or belt sanders. "The majority of folks who take our classes want to learn about hand tools. That differs us from other [woodworking] schools," Schnobrich says.

The coffins are assembled with screws and glue, with birch plugs to cover the screw holes. Wooden cross members are attached across the width of the bottom to tie the sides together and provide extra strength. The lid is made of several boards glued together, then cut to fit the top of the box; some students prefer a hinged lid, while others don't. Birch handles are attached to the full length of the coffin on each side. When one student decided she wanted round handles, Schnobrich drove out to a friend's woods and cut several small spruces, which he and the student peeled by hand and turned into handles.

What if you're not planning to use the coffin in the immediate future? According to the school's course description, "the above-ground applications are numerous, including bookshelves, a coffee table, a storage container or entertainment center, not to mention a great conversation piece."

State Laws for Do-It-Yourself Burials

The Minnesota Department of Health regulates the burial and funeral industry, though some counties and municipalities have additional codes. Here are some state regulations, available on the health department's website:

» Minnesota law does allow for burial in handmade caskets, but burial of a body must be in a legally registered cemetery.

» Burial on private property is allowed in some cases, but it is necessary to establish a private cemetery on the private property. A private cemetery typically must be surveyed, mapped, and registered with the county or city with jurisdiction. Local zoning laws need to be consulted before burial.

» State law requires a body to be buried or cremated "within a reasonable amount of time." If embalming is not desired, a body must be buried or cremated within seventy-two hours after the body is released from the place of death or by the coroner or medical examiner. Refrigeration can extend the period.

» A disposition permit is required prior to burial, entombment, or cremation of a body. The disposition permit is issued by the state registrar.

BWCA Skills Everyone Should Know

THERE IS NO BETTER PLACE in Minnesota to test backcountry travel and woods skills than in the Boundary Waters Canoe Area Wilderness (BWCAW). In addition to knowing how to canoe, you'll need to master the basics of packing light, cooking over a stove or campfire, and using camping and possibly fishing gear. Many books have been written on the subject; here are a few basics.

Basic Canoe Skills

» TWO PEOPLE MOVING FORWARD. To be efficient, paddlers should pick opposite sides for paddling a tandem (two-person) canoe. When either person tires of one side, the paddler should say "switch" and change sides. Try not to switch too frequently; it can slow the canoe and throw the stern paddler off course. An example of inefficient switching is paddling twenty times on one side and three times on the other. Learning to be a strong paddler on both sides of a canoe will make you a more popular paddling partner.

When it comes to steering a tandem canoe in most flat-water conditions, the stern (rear) paddler should take the lead and guide the direction of the canoe. The bow (front) paddler provides consistent forward power and helps the stern paddler identify obstacles like rocks.

Good communication between the bow and stern paddlers is required to keep the canoe going forward efficiently. If the bow paddler is making direction corrections independently, the canoe's path across the lake may resemble a zigzag and not a straight line.

» MASTER THE J STROKE. Every stern paddler needs to know how to keep the canoe going straight. One way is to learn the J stroke, a fundamental, forward stroke that ends with a steering maneuver. It keeps the canoe moving forward while providing a slight course correction at the end of the stroke. If you learn the J stroke and incorporate small course corrections with each stroke, you don't have to make big, energy-wasting strokes to keep going straight.

To make the top of the J, reach forward with the paddle, plant it in the water, and draw it toward your hip. Keep your arms and upper body relaxed. When the paddle reaches your hip, begin making the bottom of the J by turning the shaft so the front (power) face of the paddle is facing away from the canoe. Finish the bottom of the J by pressing the front paddle face outward against the water. The bottom of the J doesn't have to be an intensive muscle move. It should be slight and not wearing. The key is using several J strokes to make your course directions.

Some paddlers prefer pressing the paddle's shaft against the canoe's gunwale (top edge), using it as a fulcrum for added leverage at the bottom of the J stroke. It does save wear and tear on your joints. Other paddlers, however, don't like the shaft banging on the side of the canoe or wearing against the gunwale and let their wrist and shoulder bear the resistance.

» MAKE YOUR PADDLING EASIER. Here are some tips for paddling without wearing yourself out:

Don't keep a death grip on your paddle. Keep your hands relaxed.

Pick a paddle that is the right size for you. Ask your outfitter or retail salesperson to properly size you for your paddle. If you're small, don't pick a paddle blade the size of Texas. If you played sports in college and can move some water with your blade, don't pick a tiny paddle blade. Your partner will appreciate the added power.

Keep your map in a waterproof sleeve and visible while you're paddling. Learn to line up landmarks with your map. Good map reading will keep you from making navigational mistakes.

No matter the temperature, drink plenty of water while paddling. Your energy level will stay high and so will your good cheer.

A properly fitted life jacket is a must. There is nothing worse than a chafing or binding life jacket to take the fun out of paddling.

❱❱ LOADING YOUR CANOE. If you frequently occupy the stern of a canoe, you'll notice that an unbalanced load of Duluth packs makes it more difficult to steer. With an unbalanced load, you might also notice the boat leans more to one side. For these reasons, you should take a bit of extra time to make sure your packs and their weight are distributed evenly in the boat.

Once you find a well-balanced arrangement of your packs (for instance, the food pack on the left, the tent and kitchen pack on the right, your clothes pack at your feet), load the canoe the same way each time. It will improve the rhythm of your portaging and keep your canoe balanced each time you step into it.

Keys to a Good Night's Sleep

Out in the wilderness, a few important steps will help ensure a restful night:

❱❱ Make sure your tent site is level and clear of roots and rocks. Before pitching your tent, visualize yourself sleeping in that spot. Do you really want your head bumping against that giant white pine stump? Before I pitch the tent, I sometimes lie down in my future sleeping spot to gauge its levelness and smoothness.

❱❱ Bring a sleeping bag pad that fits your length and meets your comfort expectations. You might save a few ounces in weight with a short pad, but who cares if you can't get a good night's sleep?

❱❱ Bring a small camp pillow. There are good ones on the market these days.

❱❱ The best way to stay warm on a cool night is to wear a lightweight stocking cap.

❱❱ Bring a pair of silicon ear plugs. It's good insurance against heavy snorers in your group.

Encouraging Your Canoeing Partner

№ 6

If your spouse or romantic partner doesn't wholly embrace the Boundary Waters Canoe Area Wilderness experience, here are some tips:

Couple canoeing with dog, 1910

›› Be sure that he or she has the best life jacket and insect repellant money can buy.

›› Pack in fresh food for your first dinner on the trail. A fresh Cobb salad or grilled porterhouse steak is a treat your partner won't forget.

›› If you're bringing dehydrated food, invest in a quality brand. Ask experienced campers which brands and individual meals they prefer.

›› Don't forget to bring your partner's favorite beverage, whether it's expensive South American coffee or a favorite beer or wine. (The latter two can be purchased in plastic containers to comply with the wilderness no-glass rule.)

›› Surprise him or her with dessert. Freeze-dried ice cream is a lightweight and novel choice.

›› Expensive chocolate bars can really brighten a rainy day. Even better when they're a surprise.

›› Make sure to bring a high-quality headlamp for late-night trips to the latrine.

›› Don't skimp on sleeping pads. Buy the thick one for your partner. A restful night's sleep in the Boundary Waters pays dividends.

›› Love notes hidden in their Duluth packs or next to their sleeping bags are always a good way to start or end the day.

» Do your due diligence and make your camp bear- and storm-proof before you go to bed.

» If you're properly hydrated during the day, you won't go to bed with a splitting headache.

Changing Diapers

It's not unusual to see diapered children in the Boundary Waters. The key is to accurately judge the number of diapers you'll need and to pack out the soiled ones. Keep clean diapers handy at the top of a Duluth pack and dedicate a special plastic bag and a compression stuff sack for soiled diapers. Put only biodegradable wipes and paper—not diapers—in the latrine.

Twelve Ways to Wait Out a Windy or Rainy Day

1. Read Henry David Thoreau or Sigurd Olson to each other.
2. Play poker using M&Ms as poker chips. Eat them after each hand.
3. Cut extra firewood for the next group that uses your campsite.
4. Whittle a wooden spoon.
5. If you have kids along, build a tiny village with twigs and populate it with pinecone people.
6. Gaze into the campfire and meditate.
7. Master new rope knots.
8. Nap as long as you want.
9. Pull out your maps and consider future routes. Memorize lake names.
10. Rearrange your fishing tackle box or first-aid kit.
11. Make each other laugh with stories from high school.
12. Pick up and dispose of all those small bits of rope, paper, wrappers, and anything else left by other campers that accumulate around campsites.

Portaging Etiquette

IN THE BOUNDARY WATERS CANOE AREA WILDERNESS, portages are trails that provide critical travel connections between lakes and rivers. Portages are areas where wilderness travelers frequently meet, and because the portages and landings are typically not large—and some are downright narrow, rugged, and difficult to negotiate—portage etiquette is important.

Portage etiquette does not get a lot of ink in Boundary Waters guidebooks, but it can be the source of spirited discussions on the Internet and around campfires. Oddly, you can hear parallel etiquette complaints about the habits of freeway drivers and people portaging canoes—namely, lack of courtesy, going too slow, and impatience.

FAST FACTS

№ **7**   ## Basic Portaging Etiquette

1 Be organized. When you arrive at a portage, have a plan for loading and unloading your canoe. Scattering your gear across the portage is a big no-no; it doesn't leave other canoeists room to land and unload their boat. The better organized you are, the faster you will get across the portage.

2 Don't hog the landing with your canoes and gear. Keep your canoe and gear to one side and out of the way of others.

3 If two groups are sharing the portage, and one group is working faster or has less gear, it is good etiquette to allow the faster group to move down the portage first.

4 Avoid having lunch or breaks on a portage unless there is sufficient room for other parties to move past you.

5 Wait patiently in your canoe for your turn if the portage is crowded.

6 If you are on your last trip and you have a spare hand, offer to carry a piece of another party's gear. It is a gesture that someone will hopefully return.

Portaging in the BWCAW

RED PINE

NORTHERN RED OAK

SUGAR MAPLE

BALSAM

TREMBLING ASPEN

Five Minnesota Trees

Red Pine

Minnesota's state tree, the red pine is often mistakenly called a Norway pine. Red pines can grow into tall, stately trees, and some of the state's largest specimens are seen at Itasca State Park, which once was home to the world-record red pine. Red pines are known for their distinctive, puzzle-shaped reddish and orange-brown bark. Red pine is planted more than any other tree in Minnesota and is often seen in plantation-like rows.

Northern Red Oak

Northern red oaks are a large and common oak species in Minnesota, especially in the south. It is a common tree of the southern "Big Woods." It has multi-lobed pointed leaves and large acorns, and the bark is rough and generally deep furrowed. Northern red oaks are fast growers and moderately long lived, up to three hundred years. Its large, fat acorns are an important source of food for deer, squirrels, some songbirds, and wild turkeys. Wood ducks also eat the nuts. Unfortunately, northern red oaks are very susceptible to oak wilt fungus.

Sugar Maple

Sugar maples are large, slow-growing trees noted for sap that is made into maple syrup. In the fall, few trees produce more beautifully colorful leaves than sugar maples. Large stands of these maples often earn the moniker "the sugar bush."

Balsam

These medium- to large-sized trees show up every year at Christmas tree lots across Minnesota and are noted for their sweet aroma, smooth bark with resin-filled blisters, and soft branches. Balsam commonly grows across the forested parts of Minnesota but lives a shorter life than pine and spruce. Balsam is frequently turned into paper pulp, and young balsams make a tasty meal for deer and moose in the winter.

Trembling Aspen

The most abundant tree in Minnesota, the aspen is a slender tree with short branches. Its leaves are shaped like fat teardrops and appear to "tremble" in the wind. While it is a hugely valuable source of wood for the Minnesota paper industry, aspen is generally a poor choice for firewood because it burns quickly. The trees send out root suckers that grow into new trees, making aspen notable for its ability to quickly fill in newly logged areas.

FAST FACTS

№ 8

How Young?

When can I come along? Here are the ages when children can begin building their outdoor skills:

CROSS-COUNTRY SKIING: Youth ski leagues begin teaching skiing at ages four and five, but some children begin scooting around on skis as early as three.

SNOWMOBILE RACING: Youth racing, using scaled-down sleds, is open to children as young as four.

HOCKEY: Some kids lace up their skates when they are able to walk.

WATERSKIING: Strength and swimming ability are key criteria, but kids as young as four have been taught to waterski. Ages six to eight are a good time to start.

BOUNDARY WATERS TRAVEL: Skilled camping parents have taken babies into the Boundary Waters. Toddlers require a watchful eye around water and campfires.

Getting a pull at age four.

Books by Famous Adventurers and Explorers

MINNESOTA HAS AN IMPRESSIVE track record of producing explorers and adventurers, many of whom have written fine books about their quests and the skills they needed to pull them off. Perhaps it is our climate or penchant for wilderness, but a good number of native Minnesotans have penned inspiring works about Arctic travel, canoeing, and dogsledding.

» *Paradise Below Zero*, by Calvin Rutstrum. A classic, skill-filled book about winter camping and survival.

» *Winter Dance: The Fine Madness of Running the Iditarod*, by Gary Paulsen. A Minnesota native tackles one of the world's toughest overland races.

» *Hatchet*, by Gary Paulsen. A fictional account of a boy who crash-lands in the Canadian wilderness and, armed with a hatchet, lives off the land, which surely inspired legions of boys to ask for hatchets for Christmas.

» *North to the Pole*, by Will Steger with Paul Schurke. In 1986 seven men and one woman use dogsleds and their own muscles to travel to the North Pole. This book chronicles their fifty-five-day journey.

» *To the Top of the World*, by Charles Kuralt. Kuralt wasn't a native Minnesotan (though the famed television journalist owned a radio station in Ely), but he did write a fabulous book about Ralph Plaisted, the St. Paul insurance agent who snowmobiled to the North Pole in 1968.

» *No Horizon Is So Far*, by Ann Bancroft and Liv Arnesen. Minnesota native Bancroft, who was part of the Steger and Schurke expedition to the North Pole, teamed up with Norwegian Arnesen to trek twenty-three hundred miles to the South Pole.

» *Greenland Expedition: Where Ice Is Born*, by Lonnie Dupre. Using kayaks and dogsleds, Dupre and Australian John Hoelscher spent fifteen months circumnavigating Greenland.

» *The Spirit of St. Louis*, by Charles A. Lindbergh. The Little Falls native spent seventeen years writing his autobiography of the historic flight from New York to Paris.

» *The Lonely Land*, by Sigurd F. Olson. Once described as America's "best-known living woodsman," Olson canoed with five friends five hundred miles down

Canada's Churchill River. In one chapter, Olson lovingly describes how to smoke northern pike over a campfire.

» *Canoeing with the Cree*, by Eric Sevareid. The future CBS newsman never intended for this canoeing adventure with friend Walter Port to become a classic, but it did. That they canoed from Minneapolis to Hudson Bay in 1935 without any of today's modern navigation tools speaks volumes of their skills.

» *Distant Fires*, by Scott Anderson. Anderson of Duluth also canoed to Hudson Bay but began from Lake Superior.

New-Age Ice Fishing

ONCE CALLED THE "MORONIC SPORT" by author Jim Harrison, ice fishing has become big business in Minnesota, with some resorts hauling in more cash in the winter than in the summer. This is not your grandfather's ice fishing. The sport has undergone a transformation not unlike that of the telephone. Equipment has gone from big and clunky to sleek and digital. Today's ice angler is not tethered to a single spot—think of that old wall phone in your kitchen—but is comfortably mobile, linked in various ways to the outside world, and often entertained by different screens.

Ice fishing consumer shows—yes, they have their own indoor retail exhibitions— are so popular that opening day means long lines of people waiting to see the latest technology, not unlike the opening of a new Apple store.

Technology has been good for ice fishing, eliminating some of the guesswork and making a day on the ice less of an endurance test. While some anglers would never think of leaving their expensive electronic fish locators onshore, others prefer to enjoy a quiet day on the ice without fancy gizmos, entertained by a crackling wood stove and the whistle of wind across the barren ice.

The Shelter

The handmade plywood shelter has given way to thirty-thousand-dollar, aluminum-clad ice-fishing recreational vehicles, pulled behind a car or truck and outfitted with

Ice fishing gents, 1953

satellite television, kitchens, and sofas. The popular hybrid fish house can be used as a travel trailer in the summer and ice-fishing chalet in the winter. Most have hydraulic systems that can lift and lower the entire structure so it rests closer to the ice; prefabricated holes in the floor have special hatch covers for summer travel.

On a smaller scale, cloth-side fish houses are outfitted with breathable, insulated material. The portable houses can be folded up in a minute and become a sled, easily towed by hand or by all-terrain vehicle or snowmobile. The idea is to not wait for the fish in a single spot, but to move constantly until fish are located.

The Hole
You can use a hand auger, but most anglers use gas-powered augers with laser-sharpened blades that can rip through three feet of ice in fifteen seconds. The power auger has revolutionized ice fishing by making hole cutting an effortless affair; some anglers will cut two hundred or more holes in a day just to find the perfect spot with hungry fish.

The Clothing
Specialized ice-fishing pants and parkas, designed to keep anglers dry and warm while kneeling on the snow and ice, have taken the cold out of ice fishing. Boots are rated to keep the wearer warm in minus-forty-degree temperatures. If you want to shed your parka inside your fishing shelter, small, portable propone heaters the size of a large thermos bottle will keep you toasty.

The Gizmos
Electronic fish locators can detect fish down to the size of a crayon and tell the angler when the fish are preparing to bite. A new era of underwater cameras, lowered on a cable down the ice hole, keep anglers apprised as to the comings and goings of fish. Anglers use GPS and digital topographic lake maps to pinpoint fish-holding underwater reefs and mud bars. There are few secrets on the lake bottom anymore.

The Equipment
The long wooden dowel fashioned into an ice-fishing jigging stick has been replaced with carbon and graphite fishing rods outfitted with micro fishing lines made of super-strong braided fibers. Anglers can choose from thousands of varieties of

ice-fishing jigs, some made with glow-in-the-dark paint to attract fish in low-light conditions.

Where to Go

Ice fishing has an all-important and critical wild card: the thickness of the ice. Be sure to check with local bait and sporting stores for current ice conditions. While some anglers venture out on the ice as early as November, mid- to late December (depending upon the weather) is when solid, walkable ice forms.

The Twin Cities has dozens of small and large lakes brimming with panfish, walleyes, and northern pike; any bait dealer will give you tips on where the fish are biting and what to use. Minnesota's large lakes like Mille Lacs, Lake of the Woods, Upper Red Lake, Leech Lake, and Lake Vermilion have become meccas for ice-fishing enthusiasts. They also have hotels, restaurants, and fishing guides that cater to the ice-fishing crowd. Renting a fish house from a resort or guide is a popular and easy way to get onto the lake, and houses can be constantly moved to provide the best fishing action.

Catch and Fry a Walleye

I T HAS NEVER BEEN EASIER to catch a walleye in Minnesota. Because of special protective regulations, catch-and-release ethic in anglers, and restoration efforts, Minnesota's best walleye lakes are hitting on all cylinders. Still, on average among all anglers, it takes about four hours to catch a walleye in Minnesota. But anglers with better skills who pursue walleyes at choice times of the year can often bring home limits on a regular basis.

Where to Start

Two of the state's largest walleye lakes, Upper Red Lake and Leech Lake, have had populations restored through stocking programs and offer fast action even if you're a novice angler.

Special catch-and-release regulations on Lake of the Woods and Rainy Lake, two Minnesota-Ontario border waters, have protected spawning-size females, resulting in higher populations and trophy populations. Recent catch rates at Mille Lacs, the state's most popular walleye fishery, have been some of the best in a decade. Another lake with protective regulations, Lake Winnibigoshish, consistently produces excellent walleye catches and, according to locals, some of the best walleye fishing in memory.

What do these lakes have in common? They are all large and mostly shallow lakes with well-established spawning populations and areas. Long ago, these large lakes were coined Minnesota's "walleye factories" because of their ideal spawning habitat, but careful regulation of the fisheries has helped ensure a large base of spawning females.

These six lakes—Upper Red, Lake of the Woods, Mille Lacs, Leech, Rainy, and Winnibigoshish—are the crown jewels of Minnesota's walleye fishery. They're Minnesota's biggest walleye lakes, sprawling for miles across the northern part of the state and providing some of the best fishing in the Midwest or in the United States. Special regulations on these lakes are typically stringent, so anglers won't be able to keep every fish they catch. But those same regulations mean more, larger fish have been left in the lake to survive another day. Some anglers have actually complained of catching too many trophy fish.

Time of Year

A lot of ink is spilled deciphering Minnesota's best walleye lakes for the fishing opener, but we know the season doesn't end with that first weekend.

Arguably the best time of year to catch walleyes is from late May to early June. The Minnesota fishing opener lands in mid-May, just as walleyes have finished spawning, and they are still oriented to the spawning grounds along the shallow shorelines. Depending on the timing of the spawn, larger females can be in a post-spawn feeding funk, which means you'll likely be catching males that are one to two pounds. But as the water warms and food such as insect larvae and minnows become more active, walleyes throw on the feed bag. That's about the time Minnesota's large walleye lakes become walleye factories for anglers.

Boat or No Boat; Guide or No Guide

In a lifetime of walleye fishing across Minnesota, I've found only a handful of places where a person can consistently catch a walleye from shore. These places are typically

Filleting the Fish

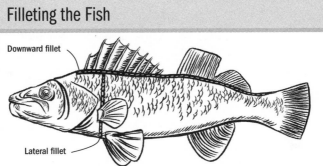

Downward fillet

Lateral fillet

GUTTING THE FISH

Some anglers prefer to gut the fish before filleting; others see it as an unnecessary step. Gutting first makes sense in the lateral fillet method because it keeps the knife from getting tangled in the offal.

To gut the fish, insert the knife in the fish's anal vent, slitting the belly forward to the gills, and remove the guts. It helps to have a source of water, such as a sink tap or hose, to wash the fish and remove slime as you fillet it.

There are two standard methods for filleting a walleye. One starts at the backbone with the knife placed parallel to the fish (downward fillet method); the other starts behind the gills with the knife placed perpendicular to the fish (lateral fillet method).

DOWNWARD FILLET METHOD

This one takes more skill. You start by laying the knife blade along the backbone and cutting downward, separating the fillet from the rib cage. Start toward the head, where the fillet is thickest, and cut the flesh away from the ribs with the knife tip while working your way toward the tail. Continue separating the flesh from the ribs as you work toward the belly. The belly fillet will be thinnest, so be careful not to cut away the fillet until you've reach the midpoint of the belly region. When you're done, you'll have a boneless fillet with skin attached. Lay the fillet on the table skin down, put the knife blade near the tail, and remove the skin from the flesh, running the blade the full length of the fillet.

LATERAL FILLET METHOD

Place the knife blade perpendicular to the fish just behind the gills. Cut downward until you feel the knife reach the backbone, then twist the blade so the cutting edge is facing the tail. Now run the knife along the backbone toward the tail, cutting the ribs where they meet the backbone. When you reach the tail, you'll have a fillet with the rib cage and skin still attached.

Place the fillet skin down on the table. Put the knife blade under the rib bones where they are thickest (along the back of the fillet), and separate the rib bones from the flesh, working toward the belly. Once the rib bones are removed, slip the knife between the flesh and skin near the tail and run the blade along the length of the fish, removing the skin.

rivers or in the Boundary Waters Canoe Area Wilderness. Sometimes you can catch walleyes from a dock early in the spring when they're oriented to shallow water. But if you're a novice walleye angler without access to one of these places, your best bet for walleyes is from a boat on a large lake.

There are many fine guides in Minnesota, and you can easily find them on the Internet and by searching individual lakes. Guides have profited immeasurably by advances in fishing technology, but a good guide will know how to catch fish when others aren't. Guides typically charge $300 to $400 a day and $200 or more per half day.

What to Use

Luckily, walleye fishing requires simple gear: a light- to medium-weight spinning rod, spinning reel, and six- to eight-pound line. While artificial bait and lures have their place in walleye fishing, the vast majority of fish are caught with live bait. A jig is a small weighted hook; the best sizes for walleye are one-eighth to three-eighths ounce. Thread a shiner or fathead minnow through the head on the jig hook, and you have a walleye catching machine, provided you keep the jig on the bottom, bouncing it lightly as if the minnow was swimming on its own. A popular live bait rig starts with a sliding sinker threaded on the line, below which is tied a swivel and a short piece of line and the hook. The Lindy Rig, popularized by fishing celebrity and expert Al Lindner, is usually slowly retrieved or trolled along the bottom. It can be tipped with a leech, night crawler, or minnow; all three are enticing bait for a walleye.

Chris's Favorite Beer Batter Recipe

Our family has a number of favorite walleye recipes, including a Thai-inspired dish, but deep-fried with a beer batter is still the number-one favorite. Ours is a two-step coating process.

Remove any bones from fillets; wash with cold water, remove excess water with paper towel, and cut into bite-sized portions.

Dust damp fillets with dry batter mix. We prefer a commercial brand, but you can make dry batters using flour and spices. Many cookbooks have batter recipes. If I'm dusting a large number of fillets and I want to save time, I put them in a sturdy paper bag with the dry batter mix and shake vigorously.

Place dry-dusted fillets in a shallow dish, being careful to keep them from clumping together or getting moist.

Meanwhile, begin to heat your oil to 375 degrees. Make sure to use enough oil to completely cover the fillets. Canola oil works well and is inexpensive, but the more expensive grapeseed is better because it reaches a higher smoke point than most oils and is healthier for you.

Prepare wet batter mix by mixing your dry batter with beer in mixing bowl. I prefer a lager, but I've used just about anything—pale ales, and even stouts—that has occupied my refrigerator. Mix your batter until it is the consistency of thin pancake batter. A mix that is too thick places too much batter on the fish; a mix that is too watery doesn't provide enough batter.

The beer's carbonation, or bubbles, in your batter is providing the exquisite light coating to your fish. The key is to beat your batter by hand enough to create bubbles, but not too much to cause them to disappear.

Dredge your dry batter fillets through the wet batter and immediately drop them in the heated oil.

Fry fillets until they are golden brown. Use a slotted spoon to remove fillets and place them in a shallow dish with paper towels between layers of fish. Use your slotted spoon to remove extra batter floating in the oil, or it will get black and begin attaching itself to fillets that are cooking.

If you are frying large quantities, keep freshly fried fillets in oven at 175 degrees until ready to serve.

Maple Syrup 101

MAPLE SYRUP conjures up images of an amber-colored liquid next to a plate of flapjacks. You might also imagine metal buckets hanging from a huge maple trunk or a rural building putting up a plume of wood smoke as sap is reduced to syrup. All of those images are apropos in Minnesota, where maple syrup producers range from backyard enthusiasts with simple pails and taps to commercial producers with vacuum hoses and large evaporators.

The Ojibwe Indians actively collected maple sap by putting a groove in the tree and catching the sap in a birch basket, then boiling the sap in wooden troughs. The Ojibwe used maple sugar as a valuable trade item. Settlers learned maple-sap collection and processing from the Ojibwe and other Native Americans across the continent. Maple processing is a uniquely North American endeavor.

In 2011, the U.S. maple syrup crop totaled 2.7 million gallons. The top producers were Vermont, New York, Maine, and Wisconsin. On a commercial scale, Minnesota is considered a second-tier maple syrup production state, but the sugar bush is very much alive and active.

The Stu Peterson Story

Stu Peterson is president of the Minnesota Maple Syrup Producers Association, a nonprofit organization "committed to the promotion of high quality maple syrup through education and information exchange." It has about 150 members, of which about 100 are from small and large commercial operators. "We have members who are very large commercial operators and others that are hobbyists. While we don't have operators on the scale of those out east, we can compete with them in terms of quality."

Peterson is a relative newbie to the business and craft of maple syruping. He was in the agricultural financing business when he retired in 2000. Though he lived in St. Paul, he loved the rural lifestyle and spent weekends visiting his lakeshore property in western Minnesota. When professional foresters assessed the timber on this property, they gave him some surprising news: he has the makings of a professional sugar bush. His maple trees were ideally suited for a small maple operation.

"I didn't know the first thing about making maple syrup, nor had much time to think about it," says Peterson of his maple knowledge prior to retirement. But he became intrigued once he learned of the foresters' suggestion, and before long he was tapping fifty trees and boiling the sap down with his neighbor, who was also new to maple syrup production. That first year they collected six hundred gallons of sap and produced seventeen and half gallons of syrup. "It was a very good year," he says.

In 2003 he and his wife built a "sugar house," a building designed to reduce sap to syrup, and in 2011 they collected 8,300 gallons of sap and produced 225 gallons of syrup on their Camp Aquila Pure Maple Syrup brand. They sell most of their syrup through retailers, both in western Minnesota and in St. Paul.

"It's a wonderful time of year to be outdoors and there is great satisfaction in producing a quality product that people enjoy," says Peterson. "It's a labor of love."

How It Works

The basics of maple syrup are this: sap is collected in late winter and early spring and then cooked over steady heat to evaporate water until only syrup is left.

It's difficult to place dates on optimal sap collection because it varies from north to south in the state and by weather. A few forty-five- to fifty-degree days with below-freezing nights should do the trick. It is normal for the flow to begin and stop as temperatures vary.

№**10** To gather the sap, a tree that is at least ten inches in diameter at chest height is chosen. A hole is drilled about one and a half feet above the ground and about two and a half inches into the tree. A simple metal tap is placed into the tree, and the sap runs out and is collected either in buckets or strong plastic bags. Producers warn against using buckets that might have contained strong-flavored foods whose taste might infiltrate the sap. If the sap is flowing, a collection bag might have to be emptied in the morning and evening.

Collecting sap, Mille Lacs, 1939

It typically takes forty gallons of sap to make a gallon of syrup, though it varies from sugar bush to sugar bush. "We usually run in the low thirties," says Peterson. "Minnesota maple trees typically have higher sugar levels." Novices often bottle their syrup in canning jars. Syrup should be heated to 180 to 200 degrees during bottling.

Minnesota has four trees that can produce sap for syrup—sugar maple, red maple, silver maple, and box elder—but sugar maple makes the best syrup because its sap is sweetest. Only backyard hobbyists tend to bother to produce syrup from the other three tree species.

You can make syrup from urban trees. Some hobbyists tap their yard trees, collect sap with small plastic jugs, and process small batches using propane cookers. "Most hobbyists have an outdoor fire pit and a flat pan. You can make some very good syrup," Peterson says. "People who do it right can do it on a small scale. Most people have a tree; they might have some experience on the farm. It's a nice time to be outside in the spring. You kind of get the bug."

A Backyard Experience

Bob White tried backyard production at his home near the St. Croix River in the town of Marine on St. Croix. He invested about two hundred dollars in equipment and tapped box elder and maple trees around his home. He reduced the sap in a turkey fryer using a propane heater and says the heating process was "incredibly inefficient," but he enjoyed the experience. He says it took about eighty gallons of box elder sap to make a gallon of syrup because sugar levels are lower in box elder trees.

"In the end, I had about a gallon and a half of box elder syrup and about a gallon of maple syrup," he says. "I kept them separate because I wanted to compare the tastes. Box elder is fruity. It doesn't have that bite that maple has. It's not as fruity as honey, but closer to honey than maple syrup," he reports. "Would I do it again? Absolutely."

Where to Learn

State and county parks often have maple syrup demonstrations, which are good places to see an operation and learn from experts. The Minnesota Maple Syrup Producers Association also has demonstrations and a handy website at www.mnmaple.org. The website has links to equipment and print resources. The town of Vergas has Maple Syrup Fest each spring with tours of sugar houses. A number of Minnesota's environmental learning centers also offer demonstrations.

The bible of maple syrup production is the *North American Maple Syrup Producers Manual*, produced and sold by Ohio State University.

Snowmobile History and Know-How

THROUGHOUT THE LAST HALF of the twentieth century, tinkers and inventers in the Snow Belt states toyed with the idea of a machine that could travel across snow where cars and trucks couldn't. While no single person can claim the title of inventor of the snowmobile, the sport of recreational snowmobiling has deep roots in Minnesota, more so than in any other state.

It began in the 1950s in the shop of Hetteen Hoist and Derrick, a Roseau metal and farm machinery shop that would later become Polaris Industries. Edgar Hetteen, considered today the grandfather of snowmobiling, started the shop with his brother-in-law, David Johnson, and younger brother, Allan.

Their shop built hoist machinery and farm equipment, and farmers counted on it to weld or fix any broken machinery. In 1955, while Edgar was on a sales trip, three company workers—David Johnson, Paul Knochenmus, and Orlen Johnson—fashioned a snow machine that would help farmers and trappers get into the backcountry. According to Polaris Industries official history, the machine used a grain elevator conveyor belt as a track. The machine was later sold to a Roseau lumberyard owner. In 1956 Allan Hetteen built the company's second snow machine. In a financial fix, the company sold that machine as well, so it could make payroll.

Throughout the late 1950s, Polaris Industries' bread and butter was still farm products, but Edgar Hetteen, who had dropped out of school in the eighth grade, began to see the possibilities of building and selling the snow machines. (The term "snow machine" was popular back then, highlighting an early view of them as rugged, utilitarian machines, but "snowmobile" was adopted later as the machines became sleeker, sportier, and faster.)

In 1960 Edgar Hetteen decided to generate some publicity for the company's slow and clumsy Sno-Traveler machine by undertaking a twelve-hundred-mile journey across the Alaska bush with three friends. The stunt not only made headlines, but it proved the machines were durable for rugged travel.

The company's directors, however, didn't like Hetteen's high-profile adventure, and their relationship fractured. Edgar Hetteen left Polaris in 1961. His brother, Allan, stayed behind and continued to lead Polaris, albeit briefly. The company refined and tinkered with snowmobile designs, producing a failed sport snowmobile called the Comet in 1963. Subsequent models called the Colt and Mustang were commercial successes, however, and the company's snowmobile business grew.

Meanwhile, Edgar Hetteen had moved his entrepreneurial efforts down the road to Thief River Falls, where he started a company called Polar Manufacturing in 1961. A year later, he changed the named to Arctic Enterprises, and its snowmobile was known as the Arctic Cat. Hetteen stepped down from leading the company in 1965 and went on to start several other successful businesses.

Today, Polaris and Arctic Cat are still Minnesota-based companies and among the four largest manufacturers of snowmobiles in the world.

Edgar Hetteen never made a fortune from snowmobiling, but he lived life as an entrepreneur with extraordinary energy. In the early 1980s, he started another company called ASV, which specialized in making rubber-tracked utility vehicles that have low impacts on the environment, and it was with ASV that he found financial success. He died in 2011 at age ninety.

Snowmobiling remains an exciting sport because today's machines are sleek, fast, fuel-efficient, and comfortable. Trail riding has become a group-oriented sport. It's common in the winter for the parking lots of rural restaurants to be filled with groups of snowmobilers, many of them entire families, enjoying a day of long-distance riding.

Perhaps the biggest appeal of snowmobiling is comfort; today you can zip across well-groomed trails on a machine with sophisticated shock absorber systems (no longer creating backaches), heated hand grips, and precision maneuverability. Today's snowmobiles are quieter, too, with some employing four-stroke-engine, gas-sipping technology that eliminates much of the complaints about snowmobiles being noisy. While there is still a segment of utilitarian snowmobiles, favored mostly by anglers, a snowmobile today is viewed as simply a fun machine to ride—to blast over snowdrifts, race across lakes, and take to the woods for long trips in comfort.

Minnesota has about 250,000 registered snowmobiles. The Antique Snowmobile Club of America is based in Minnesota, and its members fondly maintain many of the state's earliest snowmobiles, including vintage Polaris and Arctic Cat models. According to the club's sponsor, the Midwest Vintage Snowmobile Shows, the world's largest vintage snowmobile rally is held annually in Waconia, attracting thousands of enthusiasts.

Snowmobile 101: What You'll Need

» A SNOWMOBILE. You'll need a currently registered snowmobile in good working condition. Snowmobiles must meet headlight, brake, reflector, and muffler
requirements. Snowmobiles operating on state or grant-in-aid-funded trails must
have a snowmobile state trail sticker.

» CLOTHING. Today's one-piece snowmobile suits are warm, comfortable, and stylish. If you don't have a suit, you should wear layers of warm clothing topped with a
windproof outer later. Specially designed gloves, boots, and helmets are important.
Your helmet should be safety certified, fit properly, and be in a good condition. A
visor is essential. Helmets are required for riders under eighteen, except when par-
ticipating in a parade or operating on land belonging to a parent or direct relative.

» TRAINING. Minnesota state law requires residents born after December 31, 1976,
to take safety training and to have a snowmobile safety certificate. Youth safety
courses are available to riders ages eleven and older and are taught by Department
of Natural Resources–certified volunteer instructors. Adult safety training is available on compact disk as an independent study course.

» WHERE YOU CAN RIDE. In general, other than on your own land, snowmobiles are
allowed on state and local trails; iced-over waters with legal access; township roads
not restricted by local ordinance; public lands open to motorized vehicles; in the
bottom or outside slope of a ditch of county or state roads; in the same direction as
road traffic in a ditch from one-half hour after sunset to one-half hour before sunrise.

There are other restrictions that guide snowmobile riding in the seven-county
Twin Cities metro area. You cannot ride on a roadway, shoulder, or inner slope of
a ditch of a state or county road, in the median of a four-lane roadway, or within
the right of way of any interstate highway. Check state snowmobile regulations for
other restrictions.

» WHAT IS A GRANT-IN-AID TRAIL? The program collects fees from snowmobile reg-
istration, trail sticker fees, and gas taxes and funds trail development and maintenance through local clubs and groups. The volunteer groups work with private
landowners to route trails across their land. The DNR operates the program, which
is responsible for the development and upkeep of most of the state's twenty-two
thousand miles in snowmobile trails.

» SPEED LIMIT. Fifty miles per hour on any public lands or waters; the posted speed
limit on a trail; and speed limits posted by local governments or agencies.

» SINK YOUR SLED? If a snowmobile falls into a lake, it's state law that the owner must notify the county sheriff within forty-eight hours and the sled must be removed from the lake within thirty days. This also applies to cars, trucks, watercraft, and all-terrain vehicles.

Understanding Snowmobile Turn Signals

» LEFT TURN: left arm extended straight out and pointing in direction of turn
» RIGHT TURN: left arm out, forearm raised to shoulder height, and elbow bent up at ninety-degree angle
» STOP: left arm raised straight up over head
» SLOW: left arm extended out and angled toward ground

Mastering Campfires

ANYONE WHO REGULARLY BUILDS campfires has an opinion about the process for going from match to blaze as quickly as possible. I have a friend who sings the praises of copious amounts of charcoal fluid, which he calls "Boy Scout Juice." I know flame purists who wouldn't dream of using a scrap of paper as tinder, much less a liquid accelerant. Some backyard fire builders are fond of wooden matches; others like to draw the first flame with those wandlike lighters outfitted with a trigger. A key consideration is what is available to you and how far away you are from civilization. Newspaper is an excellent tinder, but you don't want to carry a bunch of newspapers on a weeklong trek through the Boundary Waters. A disposable lighter is great until it malfunctions, and you don't want that to happen while lighting a romantic beach fire.

I've built campfires in the Canadian Arctic and in Florida's Ten Thousand Islands; in the high Sierra Nevada and in the deserts of the Great Basin; in the frozen swamps of Minnesota when it is twenty below zero and in countless grates and pits in campgrounds across the United States. Becoming a campfire pro is easy if you have the right materials and follow these few guidelines:

Building a Campfire

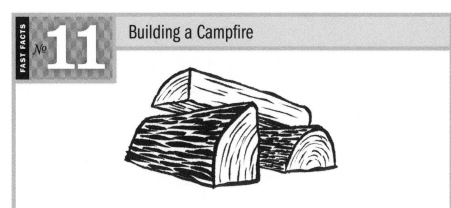

1 Pick a good spot that is dry, away from other combustible material, and exposed to good air flow. If required, always use the cast-iron grate or metal box that is provided at a campground or campsite.

2 Be a good judge of dry firewood. Use your fingers and nose. Does the wood feel or smell wet, especially after you have peeled away the bark or split it? Has it been exposed to air and aged, or has it been lying on the ground under a pile of wet leaves? Trying to start a campfire with wet wood is typically a losing battle.

3 Start with dry tinder and small kindling sticks. Tinder can be paper, dry grass, or pine needles. Put it in a pile and stack finger-length kindling around and on top of it. Be sure to leave space around the kindling to draw oxygen into the flames.

4 Light your tinder and kindling and allow time for the flames to fully ignite it. Be ready with a steady supply of larger sticks to further fuel your fire. If your tinder-and-kindling pile goes out, determine if it was wet or not getting enough oxygen and try again, perhaps with different combination of tinder and kindling.

5 Once your fire catches, add additional sticks by laying them in alternating directions so the interior of the fire can draw oxygen. Piling firewood in a parallel fashion or too densely is a sure way to starve your campfire of needed oxygen. A good strategy is to stack the wood in a vertical "teepee" design over the growing fire.

6 Monitor your fire's progress. If you add wood that hisses or smolders, it is probably wet. If you pile on too much wet wood, your fire can go out. Wet wood can burn, but only if your fire is sufficiently hot enough to ignite and burn it.

7 Coals are best for cooking—they supply the most consistent heat—so wait until your fire has been reduced to reddish coals before trying to cook.

8 Never leave your campfire unattended and always fully extinguish it before you leave your site.

When Nature Calls

HAVING TO USE THE BATHROOM where no bathroom exists isn't such an indelicate subject anymore. Entire books have been written on how to go potty in the woods. When they get their permit, every Boundary Waters traveler is required to view a video where, among other things, the issue of where to do your business is squarely explained. It's a good thing. The Leave No Trace ethic was borne out of the very real necessity to keep people's backcountry waste from piling up.

In the Woods

In the Boundary Waters Canoe Area Wilderness, the U.S. Forest Service requires campers to use campsite-specific latrines. But if a campsite latrine isn't handy, the Forest Service recommends that you dig a cathole six to eight inches deep and at least 150 to 200 feet away from lakes or streams. Chock-full of bacteria and microbes, the top six inches of forest topsoil is well suited to decompose human waste. You can dig a cathole with the toe of your boot or a camping trowel. When you're done, fill the hole with dirt and cover it with other forest floor matter, like leaves or needles. Toilet paper should be burned, provided there aren't extreme dry conditions and high danger of forest fires. Smokey Bear probably isn't thinking of flaming toilet paper when he says, "only you can prevent forest fires," but it has happened.

Because no one wants to see human excreta in the forest, the cathole technique is appropriate for any woods bathroom break, and it's the recommended leave-no-trace method by the National Outdoors Leadership School (NOLS) Wilderness Guide. NOLS recommends that larger groups using the backcountry should dig a latrine if none is available.

In a Boat

The most popular fishing boat in Minnesota is sixteen to eighteen feet long and doesn't have a bathroom. I've spent hundreds of hours in the company of fishing guides in this style of boat, and they all would gladly take a client to shore to use the restroom. But if the fish are biting, there is the coffee can method. They keep a coffee can handy for their male clients to urinate in; the can is then emptied over the side of the boat. While it isn't ideal, it probably isn't harmful to put a few ounces of urine in a lake of millions of gallons of water. I've also seen men in boats urinate into a resealable plastic water bottle and empty it back at the restroom onshore.

Female Urination Devices (FUDs)

Men can urinate while standing up. There is movement afoot to help women do the same, especially when they're outdoors, in a boat, or hanging in a climbing harness from a granite cliff. In recent years, at least a half dozen brands of female urinations devices (FUDs) have hit the market; *Backpacker* magazine, sensing a trend, even sent a crew of women into the backcountry to test and rate them. All FUDs have a similar design with a cup that tapers into a funnel with an open end. The idea is for women to stand and aim like men. One company, called GoGirl and based in Minnesota, has the motto Don't Take Life Sitting Down.

Home Pickling like a Pro

PICKLING IS a global culinary form that preserves many varieties of food, not just cucumbers. If your grandmother or great-grandmother was a pickler, it's no surprise: many immigrant groups brought their pickling traditions to the New World, whether it was kimchi from Korea, pickled herring from Scandinavia, or brined cucumbers from Europe and elsewhere. There are two basic processes for pickling: fermentation in a salt brine (sauerkraut for instance) or preservation in a vinegar brine (grandma's fresh dill pickles). Fermentation is the creation of good microbes that ward off the spoiling variety. Adding vinegar to low-acid foods lowers the pH levels so microbes that cause spoilage can't grow. Because pickling protects food from microbes that can make you sick, it is important to follow recipes closely; slightly altering the vinegar proportion in a jar of pickles could render them inedible.

Pickling is enjoying a renaissance. Debra Botzek-Linn, University of Minnesota Extension food science educator, says her agency has seen an uptick in do-it-yourselfers looking for information on pickling and home food preservation in general. In 2004 the Minnesota legislature passed the "Pickle Bill" that allowed the sale of preserved acid or acidified foods at farmers markets and community events. Vegetables from asparagus to zucchini can be pickled, as well as fish, meats, and eggs. Chutney, hot sauces, and relishes are also examples of pickling, and they can be hot, sweet, or sour, or all those flavors at once.

Changes from Your Grandmother's Day

Botzek-Linn says today's pickling guidelines are much improved over yesteryear's. She says all fresh-packed (or uncooked) pickles should be processed in a hot-water bath to destroy any acid-tolerant bacteria and to reduce spoilage. Not all home picklers used to do that. Recipes today are more consistent in requiring 5 percent acetic acid vinegar to ward off spoilage. Food scientists today also agree that alum, lime, or grape leaves are not necessary to produce crisp pickles. With today's larger refrigerators, many home picklers are drawn to the ease of making refrigerator pickles.

How to Start

Find a recipe. There are a number of fine pickling books, and the University of Minnesota Extension has a website devoted to pickling. Botzek-Linn recommends beginners start with a refrigerator pickle made with a sliced vegetable where crispness is less of a factor.

My career in pickling began one summer with a batch of kosher dill pickles and pickled green beans, commonly called "dilly beans." I grew my own green beans and purchased my pickling cucumbers (the short ones with lots of bumps) from a farmers market, where growers are increasingly finding an outlet for their products with home canners. Pickling cucumbers aren't commonly sold at grocery stores, so farmers markets or food co-ops are a good place to find them.

Instead of fermenting my cucumber pickles, I decided to fresh pack them in jars and can them using a standard hot-water bath method. I started with eight pounds of pickling cumbers. I cleaned them and cut one-sixteenth of an inch from the blossom end of the cucumber, which helps to keep pickles from becoming soft. I mixed sugar, salt, vinegar, and water in a large saucepan and added spices. You can purchase prepackaged spices or create your own, which lends creativity to your pickles. I packed the pickles in hot pint jars, filled the jars with the vinegar mixture, and made sure to leave a quarter inch of head space (the distance from the top of the liquid to the jar rim). Each jar received a head of fresh dill, a sliced jalapeño pepper, a crushed garlic clove, and a quarter teaspoon of mustard seed. The pints were sealed with lids and bands and processed for fifteen minutes in a boiling-water canner.

This is an overly simplistic recipe; the point is, pickling isn't overly complicated. My kosher dills took about two hours to prepare. Ditto for my pickled green beans. They were pretty good, too, when I cracked open the jars later that fall and winter.

There are a few key considerations to a successful pickling job. You should pickle vegetables or fruits within a day or two of picking them. Use only pure granulated canning or pickling salt, which doesn't have additives that may cloud your brine or darken pickles. Since 5 percent acidity is required, avoid any vinegar with unknown acidity. Many pickle recipes call for distilled white vinegar, which is clear with a tart acid flavor. Its advantage is that it doesn't affect the color of vegetables or fruits. Apple cider vinegar, which is fermented apple juice, is also used in recipes because of its fruity flavor, but it may darken or discolor produce.

Sugar is a common ingredient in pickle recipes; use only fine-quality cane or beet sugar. The way to discover full-flavor tastes is with spices and herbs. Whole fresh spices are preferred, though dry spices such as coriander, pepper, turmeric, cloves, and celery seed are obviously appropriate according to tested recipes.

A word about water. Soft water is a must in making brine. "Die-hard, successful dill pickle makers are very particular about the type of water they use for their pickling brine," says Botzek-Linn.

Tools You Will Need

You'll need a kettle for heating the brine, preferably stainless steel. I inherited my jars from my mother-in-law, but you can buy them in many hardware and farm stores, along with lids and rings. You'll need a funnel that helps in filling jars, a special contraption that looks like giant pliers called a jar lifter, and a wand with a magnetic tip for removing lids from hot water. Other items, like measuring cups, spoons, and spatulas, are found in most home kitchens.

Pickling Fish

Northern pike, herring, white suckers, and salmon are Minnesota fish that are commonly pickled. Pickling fish requires you first kill parasites that might have lived in the fish. In Minnesota the broad fish tapeworm is a worry, according to the university extension. There are two ways to kill the tapeworm: simmer fish in pickling brine to 140 degrees or, if you are pickling fish raw, freeze it to 0 degrees for forty hours before brining.

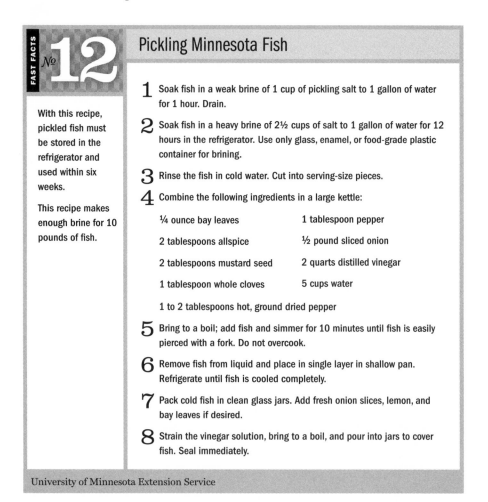

FAST FACTS

№ **12**

Pickling Minnesota Fish

With this recipe, pickled fish must be stored in the refrigerator and used within six weeks.

This recipe makes enough brine for 10 pounds of fish.

1 Soak fish in a weak brine of 1 cup of pickling salt to 1 gallon of water for 1 hour. Drain.

2 Soak fish in a heavy brine of 2½ cups of salt to 1 gallon of water for 12 hours in the refrigerator. Use only glass, enamel, or food-grade plastic container for brining.

3 Rinse the fish in cold water. Cut into serving-size pieces.

4 Combine the following ingredients in a large kettle:

¼ ounce bay leaves	1 tablespoon pepper
2 tablespoons allspice	½ pound sliced onion
2 tablespoons mustard seed	2 quarts distilled vinegar
1 tablespoon whole cloves	5 cups water
1 to 2 tablespoons hot, ground dried pepper	

5 Bring to a boil; add fish and simmer for 10 minutes until fish is easily pierced with a fork. Do not overcook.

6 Remove fish from liquid and place in single layer in shallow pan. Refrigerate until fish is cooled completely.

7 Pack cold fish in clean glass jars. Add fresh onion slices, lemon, and bay leaves if desired.

8 Strain the vinegar solution, bring to a boil, and pour into jars to cover fish. Seal immediately.

University of Minnesota Extension Service

Build a Snow Fort or Quinzhee

Snow is a remarkable and fun material for making structures, especially if you're a youngster. An annual rite of winter at my house is building a snow cave or quinzhee, which is generally defined as a snow shelter, whereas an igloo is made with blocks of ice.

Start by shoveling snow into a large mound. The larger the mound, the more people your quinzhee can accommodate. I've built quinzhees from mounds left in my driveway by the snowplow truck. You can pile snow against a wall or around a playground toy to provide an extra wall or support. Once you have a pile of snow, your

Inside a quinzhee

basic external structure is ready. Here's what to do next:

1. Allow the snow mound to harden, which can take an hour or two. The longer the mound has been allowed to "cure," the stronger the walls and ceiling will become.

2. Insert one- to two-foot-long sticks into the mound. They are guides to tell you when to stop shoveling from the inside to avoid breaking through.

3. Start by digging out the entrance. A small, short-handled shovel works best. Make the entrance large enough to crawl through.

4. Begin shoveling the inside of the shelter. It helps to have two people shoveling in an assembly line: one to clear the inside and the other to remove the excess snow from the entrance.

5. Depending upon the size of your quinzhee, you can build platforms for sleeping or extra rooms. Illuminate the inside with candles. Be sure to keep a shovel inside in case you have to dig yourself out. Walking on a quinzhee is the surest way to collapse it.

6. Even if you don't sleep in your quinzhee, there are other fun activities you can do inside, like having lunch or reading. One winter, my seven-year-old daughter and I would go outside each evening and read her bedtime story in our quinzhee. A few candles and a layer of wool blankets turned our quinzhee into a cozy reading room.

Urban Wildlife: An ID Guide

Coyotes

Coyotes live in the Twin Cities metro area, and their numbers are increasing. They are the ultimate urban wildlife survivors, sometimes living close to people and scarcely being seen. Coyotes average about thirty pounds in weight and stand about a foot and a half to two feet in height at the shoulder. They are brown and gray and have a bushy tail. They may appear bigger than their actual weight because of a thick fur coat

COYOTE

that becomes denser and fluffier in winter. Coyotes can be very vocal at night, and a single chorus of yips often starts a cacophony of howls and barks as youngsters join in. They are often seen in the suburbs, but an occasional coyote is spotted near the downtowns in brushy, riverine habitats. They are shy around humans but will prey on a vulnerable housecat or small dog. The Department of Natural Resources urges homeowners to not leave pet food outside—doing so may attract coyotes—and to keep a close eye on small pets if coyotes have been seen nearby. There are no control programs for coyotes, and they are short-lived animals. Most don't survive more than two or three years, according to the DNR, though some have been documented to live to age thirteen.

Wild Turkeys

Wild turkeys were extirpated (eliminated from their natural range) from Minnesota, but wild specimens from Missouri were reintroduced in the 1970s to the southeastern corner of the state. A trap and transplant program initiated by the DNR and the National Wild Turkey Federation succeeded in bringing wild turkeys to much of Minnesota, except portions of the northern part of the state where winters are too severe. Wild turkeys are common in urban areas today; they are

TURKEY

often seen pecking grain out of birdfeeders or traveling in flocks through neighborhoods. Some become a nuisance when they roost on roofs or become aggressive toward people. According to the DNR's website, "Habituated turkeys may attempt to dominate or attack people that birds view as subordinates." The advice here? Make sure you're at the top of the pecking order by shooing birds away and making them wary of you. Male wild turkeys can weigh up to twenty-seven pounds, and in the spring they become feathered showpieces as they puff up their feathers and strut to impress hens.

Foxes

There are two species of fox in Minnesota, red and gray, and both live in and near urban areas. Both weigh about eight to fifteen pounds and appear to be slender dogs with long, bushy tails. A gray fox has a more catlike face and is gray with light-colored belly and underfur that can be creamy or yellow buff. Gray foxes have black-tipped tails; red foxes have white-tipped tails. Both eat small mammals and birds and are normally shy of humans. Red foxes have been seen skulking along golf courses for prey, while gray foxes are seen in mature forests and woodlots. The gray fox can climb trees, either to escape danger or find prey. A gray fox once wandered into downtown St. Paul and, startled, jumped off the deck of a parking ramp. It survived.

FOX

Black Bears

Black bears are increasingly being seen in suburbs and even urban core areas of the Twin Cities. No one knows why these bears are moving toward urban areas, but it's a good guess that they are finding food (birdseed is a favorite human-provided meal) and places to hide along river and wooded corridors. The DNR does not trap and relocate urban bears; in many cases, they are shot because they pose a danger to urban dwellers and motorists. Do what you can to keep bears from your home by not leaving pet food outside or intentionally feeding them.

BLACK BEAR

Deer

Deer are commonplace in urban areas because they are adaptable to living close to people and there is plenty of food, such as acorns and tasty hostas, in urban areas. Municipalities are increasingly using limited sport hunting and professional sharpshooters to keep deer populations low; the venison from these hunts is often processed and distributed to food shelves. Deer present a real threat to motorists, and the worst time for car-deer collisions is the end of October and early November during the whitetail breeding season. Whether you live in the suburbs or rural areas, it is good to use your defensive driving skills during that period of the year. Deer travel together, so when one pops out of the ditch, another is likely following. Avoid swerving into oncoming traffic or into the ditch. You're better off hitting the deer than crashing into another vehicle or the ditch.

DEER

Opossums

Opossums have grayish fur, ratlike facial features, and a fur-less, ropelike tail. They are associated with warmer, southern climates, but opossums are increasingly colonizing urban areas of Minnesota, where they scavenge from garbage cans and find plenty of insects. In fact, opossums eat just about anything, which make them very adaptable to urban living, much like coyotes.

OPOSSUM

Firewood Cutting: For Fun and for Cabins

YOU CAN CERTAINLY BUY WOOD for your stove or fireplace, but if you own forested property or have access to some, you're missing out on a fine Minnesota tradition: cutting your own firewood. Anyone who has operated a chainsaw and felled a tree will tell you it is pretty fun yelling "*timberrrrrrr*." Bucking up a tree—cutting it into pieces—is good, fun exercise, and so too is splitting and stacking. There is tremendous satisfaction in turning a tree into a pile of neatly stacked pieces of firewood, ready to warm you when the snow begins to fly.

A few words about moving firewood: don't do it. You should cut firewood where you plan to burn it. A number of invasive insect pests, such as the emerald ash borer, that threaten the health of our forests have been introduced to Minnesota. It is now illegal to bring firewood to state lands, such as state parks, unless it is purchased from approved vendors. You can contact a local Department of Natural Resources forester for guidelines on cutting your own firewood.

Equipment: The Chainsaw

A chainsaw is the workhorse of any firewood-cutting program. Today's chainsaws are extremely reliable, are built with safety in mind, and come in a variety of sizes and bar lengths (the bar is what the chain wraps around).

When picking a chainsaw, you should consider how often you'll be using it, the size of wood you'll be cutting, and your strength. If you're cutting small branches and small trees, and you don't want to lug around a heavy saw, you'll want a small, lightweight model. The opposite is also true: pick a larger saw if you're cutting large trees and logs and if you're capable of toting a heavier saw.

Today's electric chainsaws are popular for small jobs or for people not comfortable using gas-powered equipment. I own a gas-powered Stihl MS 290, known as the Farm Boss, with an eighteen-inch bar. According to Stihl, it is their number-one-selling chainsaw because of its versatility. It's a midsized saw with plenty of power that can be used for anything from cutting brush to felling trees.

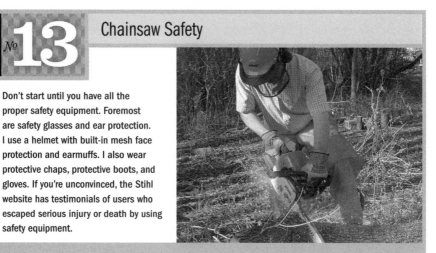

FAST FACTS

*N*º **13**

Chainsaw Safety

Don't start until you have all the proper safety equipment. Foremost are safety glasses and ear protection. I use a helmet with built-in mesh face protection and earmuffs. I also wear protective chaps, protective boots, and gloves. If you're unconvinced, the Stihl website has testimonials of users who escaped serious injury or death by using safety equipment.

Safety gear is essential for tree felling and log bucking

Other Equipment

Invest in a good long-handled splitting ax and maul. The ax is good for splitting small log rounds or kindling. A maul is a heavy, blunt ax used for big and gnarly log rounds. A maul can have an eight- to twelve-pound head, which delivers a powerful blow to any chunk of uncooperative firewood. A splitting wedge is simply a maul head without the handle that you pound into a log to split it. You may want to purchase a short-handled ax, good for cutting kindling. For tree felling, felling wedges are used to help shim a standing tree and direct it to fall in a desired direction. A few well-placed wedges can make the difference between a successfully felled tree and one that lands on the barn. Felling wedges are made of plastic, so they won't dull your saw chain.

Picking a Tree for Felling

There are lots of reasons to cut down a tree. Maybe you're tired of the leaves it drops on your deck, or your woods need a little thinning. Perhaps your tree or trees are starting to die from disease. These are all fine reasons for cutting trees, and your secondary reason may include firewood. But if you're cutting a tree for firewood, you should consider a few things. If it is alive, are you willing to wait a year until the wood is cured and suitable for burning? If it is a dead tree, is the wood still viable for burning? Finally, is it a species of tree that will produce good heat? Here are some things to consider when picking trees:

» LIVE TREES: A live tree, once cut, needs suitable time to cure before it's good for burning. Plan on curing green firewood for about a year before burning it.

» DEAD TREES: Dead standing trees can make great firewood, provided the wood hasn't become "punky," or soft. Standing dead birch, for example, can be as soft as mashed potatoes, but if cut early before the rotting process and left to dry, birch can be an excellent firewood.

» BTUs: Different species of trees generate different heating values. Go online and check on the level of BTUs (British Thermal Units) that different species can produce per cord of wood. Basswood, for instance, produces about half the BTUs per cord as white oak.

Felling 101

The key to felling any tree is to do it safely without damaging property or hurting yourself. It goes without saying you shouldn't be felling trees if you've been drinking alcohol or taking drugs or if you're tired. Good judgment and physical coordination are essential.

Every tree wants to fall in one direction; you may have other ideas. Your job is to accurately judge the "lean" of a tree and what obstacles stand in the way, such as branches. Wind can play a role, too. I own a grove of tall red pines that I'm continually thinning. On windy days, they can sway in directions I don't want them to fall. I avoid cutting on days like that.

Clear any brush from around the trunk where you can stand, and plan an escape route in case something goes wrong. Next, pick the spot where you want the tree to fall by matching the lean of the tree to a spot without any obstacles. Now cut your felling notch, which helps the tree fall in the direction you've determined. The felling notch uses two cuts. Start by making a cut parallel to the ground about half to a third into the trunk. About six to ten inches above the cut, make another one downward, meeting the inside cut of the first. You can further help direct the fall of the tree by pounding one or two wedges into a cut behind your felling notch. There are several brands of "felling" wedges, usually made of plastic, on the market.

Go to the other side of the tree and begin your felling cut about two to five inches above the wedge. Cut parallel to the ground toward the top of your felling notch. As the tree begins to fall, turn off the saw and step away. You don't need to cut completely through to your felling notch. The remaining attached wood works as a hinge or pivot, keeping the trunk from popping backward while guiding the tree toward the ground.

One risk is having the tree tilt backward, pinching the bar of your chainsaw. This is major trouble. If your saw bar becomes pinched badly, the chain and the saw will stop. Now you have a half-cut tree and your saw is stuck in it. The best way to avoid this is to judge accurately the lean of the tree and to constantly gauge your felling cut and any pinching. If you feel the slightest pinch in the bar, back out of your cut and reassess the situation. You can extract a stuck saw by pounding felling wedges into the cut. Make sure the saw is turned off.

On the Ground

Now the hard work begins. I always limb the tree next, pausing occasionally to clear away debris and limbs so I have a good work space. Once the limbing is done, you can start cutting the tree into rounds, or "bucking" up pieces that will be split. Rounds should be cut into lengths that fit your stove. Make sure your saw doesn't touch the ground while you cut logs into rounds; touching even loamy soil will dull your chain. Try to cut rounds so that knots—where limbs were attached to the tree—are at the cut edge of a round, which will make it easier to split the round.

Splitting

If you like the exercise and you have a manageable pile of rounds, a maul is the best splitting tool out there. If your pile is large and you're serious about wood as a heat source, rent a hydraulic wood splitter or, better yet, buy one. Hydraulic wood splitters take the brute strength out of wood splitting, and they're easier on your back.

If you're OK with hand splitting, an ax is good for cutting small rounds, but ultimately a maul saves time as you work through a pile of rounds. To effectively split a round, make sure you put it on a solid surface, not on the spongy ground, to get the most power out of your whack. I use a tree stump with a flat surface that is next to my woodpile. When you're ready to split, size up the round for any knots or uneven grain. These add to the difficulty of splitting and are the tough customers I set aside for special attention. If the easy, straight-grain pieces look like they'll break in half with one whack, I like to work through them first.

Large rounds also take special attention. Instead of whacking them down the middle, attack them at the sides, cutting off half-moon slices until you're ready to hit the heart with a mighty blow. Once a large round has been reduced to its inner rings, it will usually give up the ghost with one or two blows.

There are many ways to stack wood, but a few principles apply. Keep your woodpile slightly elevated off the ground with a row of boards or sticks so air can circulate under the pile, keeping it dry. It is good to keep your woodpile under cover and out of the rain, which was why woodsheds were invented. If you don't have a shed, cover the wood with a sheet of plastic or a tarp. It will keep your hard-earned woodpile dry and free of snow.

Raising and Showing Champion Dairy Cows

REID STRANSKY IS the fourth-generation farmer to raise dairy cows and grow crops on his family farm called Stranshome. Starting when his grandfather arrived in the Owatonna area from Prague in the 1890s, the Stransky family has continuously operated the farm. "I believe there have been dairy cows on the farm since the beginning," says Reid.

The Stransky family doesn't raise ordinary dairy cows. Their red-and-white and black-and-white Holsteins are blue-ribbon winners and eight-time grand champions at the Minnesota State Fair. They compete on bigger stages, too. Shows devoted to dairy cows are big business in the United States, and the biggest stage is the five-day World Dairy Expo held annually in Madison, Wisconsin. It is a sort of Westminster Kennel Club dog show for milk cows. In 2009 the Stranskys' champion red-and-white Holstein, Nan, won her class at the World Dairy Expo but was also unanimously named an All-American for her breed, meaning she was the nation's best. (She was a grand champion and awarded "best udder" for her breed at the Minnesota State Fair.) "Nan is definitely the high point of our showing career," Reid says.

Reid Stransky explains dairy cow showing and how to raise a prize-winning cow.

» WHY SHOW COWS? Showing cows is big business. It does two things: it showcases your cattle, but if they do well, just like a racehorse or well-bred dog, they are valuable. There are lots of people who will pay a lot of money for top cows; some just like showing as a hobby, and they buy expensive show cows. Don Rottinghaus, a major franchise owner of Subway sandwich stores, loves to show cows. The owner of the Vancouver Canucks hockey team buys a lot of show cows every year. It's basically the same thing people do with show horses. It's a hobby and it's very intense. It's a fun nucleus of people. Some of my best friends in the world are people I met while showing cows. It's a neat group of people. My father exhibited at the Minnesota State Fair in the late 1960s and 1970s. We've shown up there on and off ever since.

» IS IT PROFITABLE? We try to merchandise these cows and their offspring. Obviously, like any dairy farm, the milk check is a big part of our business, but merchandising our cattle is 20 percent of our business. We came to a point where we decided not to expand to more milk production and to get more involved in merchandising registered cattle. It takes fewer employees. It's less work than expanding your milk production.

» WHAT BREEDS DO YOU SHOW? We breed and show mainly four breeds. We are mostly a Holstein operation, red and white and black and white. We own and show a few Jersey cattle and a few Brown Swiss.

» WHAT'S IT TAKE TO RAISE A CHAMPION COW? There are four or five factors. Before she's born, it is her genetics. What were father and mother like? We strive to show cows with good physical features. They are tall, long, and stylish. They are not fat or obese, but streamlined and thin. They are also judged on their mammary system. How high and wide is the udder? You try to find a cow with all those attributes.

» Talk about the importance of breeding. In the 1950s and 1960s, farmers started using artificial insemination. They identified the best bulls, began taking their semen and selling it. Today, we keep track of how each bull produces high-scoring offspring. There is a scoring system. For a bull's daughters, it's their milk production that is scored for the butterfat and protein content. Each bull's off-spring can be evaluated on their conformation and milk production. A lot of people watch the results of the big dairy shows to try to determine which bulls are producing quality offspring. There is a bull called Goldwyn; he is the best bull in the history of the breed. His daughters are dominating the show circuit. There also is new technology using in-vitro fertilization where you can ensure that a cow produces all heifers. Instead of one offspring, from the best bull and dam, you can have up to ten sisters. You have one versus ten. That is all we do with the show cows these days. The heifers are so much more valuable than bulls. A bull calf is worth $300 to $400; a heifer calf can be worth $2,000. It's a no-brainer to use that technology.

» Does the special care start when they are young? Yes, once the calf is on the ground, just like any best athlete, you take better care of them. It is exercise and conditioning. You want to keep them on a healthy, nutritious diet and have them live in a clean, healthy facility. You have to have the right facilities and right feed and diet for the calf to reach its full potential. All the time as they are growing you analyze them and look for good prospects. With every new crop of calves, you study them and you think, "This one could be it."

» How important is handling the cow during the show? It's an important part of the show. You get two minutes, and they have to be a good two minutes. The cow can't be moving in circles. A good showman has to know the cow well. You can make her walk a certain way and take short steps. Some guys are geniuses, heads and shoulders above the other people when it comes to showing their cows. There is a small group of people in the show world who are very successful. Part of that is having the cow broke to lead. To show a cow, you have to break it to lead. That requires ten to twenty hours of practice for a cow to follow on a lead. The other part is grooming.

» DESCRIBE THE GROOMING PROCESS. If a cow looks a little too heavy, you can clip her hair shorter. If she looks too light and she is not as heavy, you can clip her a little longer to make her look heavier. You don't want her to be swayback like a horse. You want a nice top line. You put hair spray on to hold the hair up and clip it. The haircut is vitally important. Good hair starts with a lot of washing at home. We wash our cows a lot. Like any human hair, if you don't wash cow hair for three days, it gets oily and sticky. We wash their hair to keep it healthy so it's easy to groom.

» WINNING AT THE WORLD DAIRY EXPO MUST BE EXCITING. It's very exciting, a great accomplishment. How is the Minnesota State Fair compared to the World Dairy Expo? It's like winning the conference championship compared to winning the national championship. There are 2,400 to 2,600 cows there, and it attracts all the bigwigs in the show business. Winning the World Dairy Expo is the national championship. You strive for that every year. Like any college team, you want to be national champion every year. Every year, we strive to have another All-American cow. It doesn't happen all the time. We're fortunate to accomplish that.

Tasteful Taxidermy

FOR MOST PEOPLE, the word *taxidermy* conjures images of dusty, faded deer heads hanging in a barbershop or tired-looking fish mounted over the fireplace. The idea of taxidermy as a legitimate piece of art or furniture seems preposterous as well, especially to spouses whose excited husbands shoot the buck of a lifetime and want to hang it over the couple's bed.

Betty Gaston of Taxidermy Unlimited has heard a lot of similar stories. Her husband, Marv, is a taxidermist par excellence. For fifty years, he has plied his trade in Burnsville. His shop, with seven employees, is one of the most respected taxidermy studios in America. Marv Gaston's work has earned numerous best-of-show awards in international competitions and can be seen in dioramas in Cabela's and other retail stores around the country. Clients from around the world ask him to produce life-size

Taxidermy as a part of family life, 1910

elephants, zebras, and other creatures. While his client list and reputation have grown, Marv says his philosophy on taxidermy has never wavered from the simple statement on his business card: "Preserving memories."

"You see it on the faces of kids especially," he says. "I don't care if it's their first pheasant or a ten-inch bluegill, it's nothing but smiles when they come in to pick it up. They will cherish it more than any battery-operated toy they'll ever own."

Decorating with Artful Taxidermy

Betty says the key to artful taxidermy is making sure the animal (or animals) is suitable for the size of the room and location. "The first thing we ask is, 'where is the piece going?'" Betty says. "Will it be in a trophy room and in a smaller living room?" She says the ceiling height and configuration of the room will determine how the animal is mounted. A pose called a "partial sneak" is better for rooms with lower ceilings because the animal's neck is posed forward and the head will extend from the wall, as if the animal were curiously looking ahead. A full upright pose might require more ceiling height because the animal's neck and head are upright, as if the animal were alert and looking for danger. "This is important for larger animals like elk," Betty says, "but not as important for white-tailed deer, which aren't as big and don't take up as much room."

If a spouse or partner in the home isn't fond of taxidermy, she invites them to the studio for a better look at the animals and the studio's portfolio. That often changes minds. "This will become like a piece of furniture or accent piece in your home," she says.

A new style puts the animal mount on a movable pedestal. The pedestal gives the animal more of a three-dimensional feel; the pedestal can also be moved to fit in different spaces and decors. A wall pedestal is another style, except the pedestal mounts to the wall instead of remaining freestanding.

Animals today are also being mounted together in groups in scenes that reflect the species' native habitat. It gives the animal a more natural look, instead of appearing awkwardly from the wall.

Taxidermists today are also aware that animals are sometimes used in smaller spaces. They can make antlers detachable so they can be easily carried in and out of the house. Other clients, however, are building a permanent collection that stays with the home, Betty says.

Marv has some advice, too. The "attitude" of the preserved animal—whether it is relaxed, intent, or aggressive looking—has a huge impact on its suitability for a room. "A North American mountain lion can look at ease or look intent," he says, "but I don't suggest that it is growling, howling, or hissing. If you have a mountain lion that is hissing, there is no sound coming out of its mouth. Besides, if you invite someone who is a non-hunter to dinner, they'll probably not like that kind of pose."

Still, taxidermy is a matter of personal taste, and couples often have to come to agreement on where a piece will reside in their house. Sometimes it's even more fractious than that. Marv recalls a client who had a "beautifully" mounted pheasant, but when he arrived with his girlfriend to pick it up from the studio, the girlfriend informed the proud hunter that the pheasant wouldn't be allowed in their house. Marv took the client back to his paint booth for a man-to-man talk. "I've met a lot of guys like you," Marv told the man, "and this is not the gal you want to marry. She won't let you hang up this pheasant because she doesn't like this part of your life." Marv gave the man his business card and invited him back to the studio. A little over a year later, the same man returned to introduce his new fiancée, who apparently appreciated the beautifully preserved pheasant. "I knew that other gal just wasn't going to work out," Marv says with a chuckle.

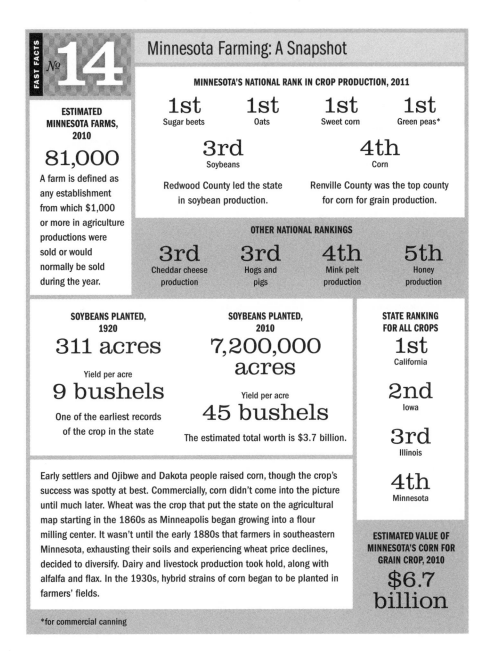

FAST FACTS

No **14**

Minnesota Farming: A Snapshot

MINNESOTA'S NATIONAL RANK IN CROP PRODUCTION, 2011

1st
Sugar beets

1st
Oats

1st
Sweet corn

1st
Green peas*

3rd
Soybeans

4th
Corn

Redwood County led the state in soybean production.

Renville County was the top county for corn for grain production.

OTHER NATIONAL RANKINGS

3rd
Cheddar cheese production

3rd
Hogs and pigs

4th
Mink pelt production

5th
Honey production

ESTIMATED MINNESOTA FARMS, 2010

81,000

A farm is defined as any establishment from which $1,000 or more in agriculture productions were sold or would normally be sold during the year.

SOYBEANS PLANTED, 1920

311 acres

Yield per acre

9 bushels

One of the earliest records of the crop in the state

SOYBEANS PLANTED, 2010

7,200,000 acres

Yield per acre

45 bushels

The estimated total worth is $3.7 billion.

STATE RANKING FOR ALL CROPS

1st
California

2nd
Iowa

3rd
Illinois

4th
Minnesota

Early settlers and Ojibwe and Dakota people raised corn, though the crop's success was spotty at best. Commercially, corn didn't come into the picture until much later. Wheat was the crop that put the state on the agricultural map starting in the 1860s as Minneapolis began growing into a flour milling center. It wasn't until the early 1880s that farmers in southeastern Minnesota, exhausting their soils and experiencing wheat price declines, decided to diversify. Dairy and livestock production took hold, along with alfalfa and flax. In the 1930s, hybrid strains of corn began to be planted in farmers' fields.

ESTIMATED VALUE OF MINNESOTA'S CORN FOR GRAIN CROP, 2010

$6.7 billion

*for commercial canning

Making Homemade Sausage

CRAIG AND DIANNE PETERSON are married, for better or for wurst.

The Grand Marais pair are Minnesota's First Couple of sausage making. Craig says his family began making Swedish potato sausage a century ago, but it wasn't until the last fifteen years that he and Dianne were asked to share their sausage-making skills. For years, they demonstrated sausage making at Farmamerica, the Minnesota Agricultural Interpretive Center near Waseca, using 1920s-vintage equipment. Today they teach about a dozen sausage-making classes annually around the state, either at the North House Folk School in Grand Marais or at Cabela's stores. Their classes are usually filled, and demand is growing because people are interested in making their own food with natural ingredients and free of chemicals, Dianne says.

"People are demanding to know what's in their food," she says. "We get a lot of students who love sausage but say they won't buy it because they don't know what's in it."

"It's a sign of the times," says Craig. "People are going back to nature. They're interested in doing things naturally and on their own."

There is an ever-increasing demand by hunters to utilize their own game to make an economical, tasty sausage. The Petersons have made sausage out of almost any meat you can think of, from Rocky Mountain sheep to fish to goose and even kangaroo. The Petersons say students are often surprised by how easy it is to make fresh, homemade sausage and to create new variations by using different spices. Here is a look into their world of kielbasas, brats, and chorizo.

Equipment

Novice sausage makers can easily get outfitted with $500 or less in equipment. The price of meat grinders and sausage stuffers rises with the capacity of the equipment to turn out bigger batches. Depending upon motor size, electric home meat grinders can cost as little as $170 to as much as $800 or more. Sausage stuffers—the machine that puts the meat into the casing—can cost as little as $125 to as much as $350. Used equipment can be found for less, and some sausage makers use hand equipment that is slower but makes fine sausage nonetheless.

"We have a friend who did a whole deer with a hand grinder," says Craig. "My family got by for a century with a stuffer that handles only five pounds at time." Other equipment includes mixing tubs, a meat scale, measuring cups, and knives.

Ingredients

Most sausage is made by mixing lean meat with fat (or fatty meat) and spices. A batch of Craig's family potato sausage included twenty-four pounds of pork (which

FAST FACTS № 15 — Know Your Sausage

BOCKWURST: A mildly spiced pork and veal sausage traditional in Munich and associated with Oktoberfest, bockwurst is flavored with onions and parsley and is prepared fresh or partially cooked.

BRATWURST (above): A bratwurst is a German-style sausage that is lightly seasoned, is made with pork, and is thicker than a hot dog. It comes in many different varieties.

BRAUNSCHWEIGER: A German sausage made with pork liver and smoked after it is cooked.

CHORIZO: A fresh sausage originating in Spain, chorizo is spicy and usually cooked before eating, but sometimes it is smoked or dried.

FRANKFURTER: A cooked and smoked sausage, usually called a hot dog, it is the most widely eaten sausage in the world. Named after the city in Germany, the frankfurter is served on a bun.

ITALIAN SAUSAGE: A fresh sausage that is both sweet and spicy, Italian sausage is spiced with coriander or fennel. It must be cooked.

KIELBASA: A thick sausage originating in eastern Europe, the kielbasa (which is Polish for *sausage*) is made with coarse-ground pork and is uncooked or smoked.

KNACKWURST (or knockwurst): A short, fat frankfurter is made of pork and beef and typically strongly flavored with garlic.

LIVERWURST: A sausage made with finely ground pork and pork liver and packed in a non-edible casing.

SALAMI: A generic name for hard, dried sausages that come in many sizes and shapes.

SUMMER SAUSAGE: A cured sausage, often called cervelat, that typically doesn't have to be refrigerated, summer sausage is made with beef or beef and pork. It's made in the summer, hence its name, and is sweeter than salami.

contained the fat), eight pounds of ground beef, and twenty pounds of potatoes. Venison is typically made with 30 to 70 percent lean meat and the rest pork. Ground pork butt, a fatty cut of pork from the hog's haunch, is a good choice for adding fat to sausage. Spices are too numerous to list here. When the Petersons teach their classes, they will spread out thirty to forty spices on a table and discuss how each can be used in sausage. Swedish potato sausage includes a standard list of sausage spices: white pepper, salt, garlic powder, allspice, and ginger powder. Dianne suggests buying spices in bulk from co-ops or health food stores to get the freshest spices possible.

Sausage can also include fruits like apples or berries, such as cranberries, and other fillers like wild rice or bread. "We don't use pre-packaged ingredients," says Dianne. "We'd rather tweak our recipes with fresh spices. We do not use MSG or anti-caking agents or preservatives."

"We make a chicken and wild rice breakfast sausage that will knock your socks off," says Craig. "We stress that sausage making is not a science, but an art form."

The All-Important Casings

Casings are the tubes that hold sausage together, unless you're making bulk sausage. Yes, natural casings are made from animal intestines, but don't worry, they're thoroughly cleaned and flushed when you purchase them fresh from your butcher. Sheep casings are the smallest of natural casings and are typically used for hot dogs or breakfast sausage. Hog casings are the gold standard for larger sausages. They come in several sizes and are used for bratwurst, knockwurst, and other large sausages. Collagen casings are made from edible protein and are used for sausage, as are some types of artificial casings, but the Petersons prefer natural casings because they make tastier sausage.

Putting It All Together

Sausage is made by mixing meat, fat, and spices in a pan, then grinding the mixture, sometimes more than once. The Petersons recommend making small batches at first and frying the ground mixture to see how it tastes. This mix and taste method in small batches avoids the hazard of making a large batch and having the mixture taste terrible. After frying the mixture, you can adjust the seasonings and make either bulk packages or patties or stuff into casings. For the latter, mixture is fed into the entire length of the casings, and individual links are twisted and separated. The sausage can be frozen or cooked fresh. The Petersons recommend refrigerating the sausages overnight to allow the flavors to mix thoroughly before cooking or freezing.

Learning How

The Petersons recommend taking a class. Otherwise, there are DVDs on sausage making and good books that cover the subject. They key is to experiment with small batches and not get in over your head and make large-scale mistakes.

"One guy we know turned his whole deer into summer sausage," says Craig. "He started with the most difficult thing," continues Dianne, "and didn't get the flavors correct." "He threw the whole thing away," says Craig.

Sing like a Voyageur

FRANCOIS FOUQUEREL is dean of the French Les Voyageurs program at the Concordia Language Village, which calls itself "the premiere language and cultural immersion program in the United States." The program's headquarters are in Moorhead, with a satellite office in Bemidji, where Fouquerel lives.

A native of Normandy, France, Fouquerel teaches French and the history of the voyageurs to youngsters every summer at the village. Les Voyageurs has a one-week and four-week program where kids camp, canoe, and learn French. Of course, the songs of the voyageurs figure prominently in the program.

Voyageurs were the freight haulers of the fur trade, says Fouquerel, an equivalent to today's semi-truck drivers who haul large loads across interstate highways. The difference, of course, is that voyageurs carried and paddled supplies, trading goods, and furs. They worked primarily for the Hudson Bay or North West Fur companies and were divided into two groups: those who traveled seasonally from Montreal to western inland trading routes and those who stayed over the winter in the north country. They were hardy, tough men, capable of carrying ninety-pound loads over difficult terrain or paddling thirty miles a day from dawn until well after sunset. Grand

Voyageurs in canoe, 1855

Portage, which was an eight-mile overland route from Lake Superior to inland water-ways, is one of Minnesota's most notable voyageur landmarks. Voyageurs traveled extensively through what is now Minnesota, and "the voyageur is definitely emblem-atic of Minnesota culture," Fouquerel says.

But why did they sing?

Songs helped ease monotonous work in many cultures, and singing likely helped voyageurs keep rhythm while they paddled. There is another theory, Fouquerel says. "Some of these voyageurs were ornery characters who signed up for a tough life," he explains. "When they were singing, they weren't arguing. It is probably a way to keep the men on task." Fouquerel says that voyageurs who could sing well often received extra pay. Unfortunately, voyageurs were mostly illiterate, and many of their songs were passed along orally and never survived. Songs were passed down through gen-erations and remain popular today, including "Alouette," "A la Claire Fontaine," "En Roulant Ma Boule," and "Frit à l'Huile."

"At the Concordia Language Villages, there are a few songs that we know that are original songs. They originated in France in the 1500s and were adapted to North American styles," Fouquerel says.

One famous song, "V'la le Bon Vent," recalls three ducks on a pond. When a prince goes hunting and aims at the black duck, he kills the white one instead. As the duck loses its blood and its feathers fly into the wind, diamonds and gold come from its eyes and beak. Three ladies gather up the feathers for a bed and invite passing men to use the bed, Fouquerel says. Such suggestive lyrics were often included in voyageur songs. "There are probably a hundred different versions of the song," he says, "and there is a lot of call and response."

The bawdy lyrics presumably entertained the men or highlight the fact that female companionship wasn't part of everyday life on the trail. Fouquerel tells a story of a group of voyageurs hired to bring some nuns to the Red River settlement. "In their contract, they were told not to sing voyageur songs because they were too raunchy for the nuns," says Fouquerel. "It turns out the nuns sang during the journey, and the guys were happy to learn some new tunes. The next season, though, the same tunes were adapted with voyageur themes."

Fouquerel says the great thing about voyageur songs is their adaptability. Verses can be added or subtracted, depending on the audience. The best songs for canoeing are those with a call and response. One singer leads with a line and the rest of the group responds. "It's very inclusive," he says. "If somebody is new to the group, all they have to do is repeat the call line. I've done it myself when the winds are against me and I'm paddling. The harder the wind, the louder you sing. When it's raining, you sing about that."

Fouquerel says voyageur songs are embedded in Minnesota history. He has heard some Catholic churches still gave mass in French in Minnesota and the Dakotas up until the 1970s. He notes that the Minnesota state seal contains the words *l'Etoile du Nord*, or "The Star of the North." When campers in the Les Voyageurs program at the Concordia Language Village take their canoe trip to the state's north country, they often sit at campsites that were likely visited by voyageurs.

"We like to remember that three hundred years ago, there was somebody else singing in French around the campfire here," he says. "We are keeping that tradition alive."

Dorisella Frances Harris Freeze knitting, 1944

Wool Wonders

How to Make Handmade Wool Socks

Julia Sandstrom has been knitting for thirty-five years. She knits while chatting with friends, at her son's wrestling meets, when there is quiet time around her Stillwater home. "I do the patterns from memory," she says. "The boys at wrestling meets are fascinated by my knitting because I can watch the meet and knit at the same time."

If you're one of Julia's friends, you'll likely have your feet measured at some point, and magically, a pair of beautiful wool socks will be delivered on your birthday or special occasion or just for friendship. "I like making socks and giving them to friends. It's a gift of love," she says.

Getting Started

You'll need practice before graduating to socks, Julia advises. Go to a knitting and yarn store and take a class or pick up an instructional book. Try making a scarf first.

FAST FACTS № **16**

Key Moments in Minnesota's Wool History

1830
At Lac qui Parle in western Minnesota, Joseph Renville reportedly owns "sheep by the hundreds and cattle by the score."

1850
According to a census, there were only eighty sheep in the Minnesota Territory, with forty-five in Ramsey County and twenty-six in Wabasha County.

1860s
Demand rises for wool during the Civil War, and Minnesota's sheep population jumps to 97,241 in 1864 and 193,045 in 1866, according to historical census reports. In September 1866, forty thousand pounds of wool is shipped from the St. Anthony railroad depot to the East Coast.

1864
The North Star Woolen Mill is built in downtown Minneapolis and produces scarves, flannels, and yards. It becomes one of the nation's largest manufacturers of wool blankets in the early twentieth century.

"While I have a friend who knitted socks as her second project, they are not something I recommend a novice knitter should try. However, socks are not that advanced either," she says.

Julia uses a basic sock pattern, knitted in the round using double point needles. "I knit on size-two needles, which are very small, sort of like knitting on toothpicks. Once you get over the shock of using small needles, it's quite easy and not so intimidating."

Picking the right yarn is key to making sturdy socks. Julia uses yarn that is 75 percent wool and 25 percent nylon. Other combinations of wool and synthetic materials work, but it is important not to use 100 percent wool. "Nylon provides some elasticity

Key Moments in Minnesota's Wool History continued

1865
Faribault Woolen Company is established on the banks of the Cannon River in Faribault.

1879
The Minnesota State Wool Growers' Association is formed.

1886 The Northwest Knitting Company
is incorporated with George D. Munsing as vice president. In 1923 it becomes Munsingwear, Inc. The company's goal is to produce woolen undergarments that would be "shaped to fit, yielding to every motion of the body yet always remaining in place."

1917
Faribault Woolen Company produces one hundred thousand olive drab army blankets for the war effort.

1920 Bemidji
Woolen Mills is founded by Ira P. Batchelder and Ira H. Batchelder to produce woolen apparel for the logging industry. The company still sells wool clothing today.

1930s
Munsingwear begins selling all-wool bathing suits.

1949
The North Star Woolen Mill moves its operations to Ohio. The building was listed on the National Register of Historic Places in 1971.

1981
Munsingwear's Minneapolis production plant closes.

1999
North Star Woolen Mill opens as luxury condominiums.

2009 Faribault
Woolen Mill closes but reopens two years later to continue making high-quality woolen products.

2011
Minnesota's sheep inventory is 130,000.

to keep the socks from falling down, but more importantly, without the synthetic material, your socks will shrink in the wash and become useless," she says.

To get the perfect fit, she traces the feet of a potential sock recipient. "I have tracings of all my friends' feet," she says. Sometimes she surreptitiously checks shoe sizes to ensure the gift is a surprise.

She can knit two pairs of adult socks and a pair of children's socks for about thirty dollars, which is essentially the cost of the yarn. If Julia asks you to stand on a piece of paper, take note: a special gift is in the works that will keep your toes toasty through the winter.

The Lake Superior Agate: Gem of the North Country

THE MINNESOTA STATE GEMSTONE was born out of the ancient lava flows (forming a rock called basalt) that can still be seen along the Lake Superior shoreline. Commonly called "lakers" by collectors, Lake Superior agates can easily be found by novice rock hounds. They can be found virtually anywhere in the state because of the mile-thick glaciers that scraped them out of the northern basalt and dumped them, mixed in with sand and gravel, across the landscape. They range in sizes small enough to fit in your pocket to twenty-pound behemoths. Their beauty is highlighted by iron—another connection to Minnesota's unique northern geology. They are beautiful enough to inspire awe and easily found by just about anyone. There are truly large and valuable specimens yet to be discovered.

In 1969 a number of rock hounds and agate fans convinced the Minnesota legislature that the Lake Superior agate was perfect for the state gemstone.

How to Find Them

Because they were moved by glaciers, agates are often found in gravel pits where aggregate and sand is mined with heavy machinery. Some very nice agates are found in gravel pits in Minnesota's Arrowhead region. Many beautiful agates are found

FAST FACTS №17 — How Agates Were Formed

Let's travel back in time about 1.1 billion years. The North American continent was splitting apart, creating a rift between two separating chunks of land. Lava pushed through the rift to the surface, spilling out in great flows that became basalt or a rock called ryholite.

Within the lava, gas bubbles formed and pushed to the surface. But some bubbles were trapped within the lava and never reached the surface and hardened. Geologists call these remaining trapped bubbles *vesicles*. Over time, the lava cracked and was infiltrated by water carrying dissolved iron, quartz, and other minerals. The minerals leached and accumulated in layers and hardened. Alternating bands of minerals were created by new introductions of mineral-rich water. The concentration of iron and amount of oxidation determine an agate's richness in color.

The resulting formations of agates were harder than the surrounding basalt. During the next billion years, the agates were freed from the rock by erosion and the scouring of glaciers. Because agates are hard, the glaciers didn't grind them up but carried them along—tumbling, cracking, and rough polishing them at the same time—until the ice melted and deposited them across what is now the Upper Midwest. Some ended up as far south as Iowa.

along creeks and riverbeds where water erosion has exposed glacial deposits. If you search for agates along Lake Superior, not all beaches contain agates. Because of the wave and ice action, most Lake Superior beach agates are small.

A handy book is *Rock Picker's Guide to Lake Superior's North Shore*, which profiles a dozen beaches for rock picking. The book ranks the Beaver River Beach as "the best Lake Superior agate beach on the entire North Shore." You can also ask at local rock shops where you should go to find agates. New agates can be exposed after storms and ice-out when wave and ice action shifts beach rubble.

What to Look For

It helps to look for agates during sunny days when the agate's quartz can appear shiny among other rocks, dirt, and rubble. Agates usually have iron oxide, which gives them a rusty, orange-and-yellow hue.

As you scan through rocks and dirt, look for the concentric mineral banding within agates that can be visible along the edges of a cracked agate.

Another clue is the pitted texture covering an agate that was created while stuck in the ancient lava flow. Some agates look as if they were molded. Some rock hounds bring a spray bottle, cloth, and even a flashlight to help reveal an agate's translucence. Sometimes a rock hound will find a specimen almost perfectly smooth. Tumbled smooth in waves along rocky beaches, these are called water-washed agates.

Minnesota Driving: A Checklist

D RIVING IN MINNESOTA requires unique skills and knowledge. Here are some things to remember:

» Don't honk at the person driving fifty-five miles per hour in the left lane, in a Toyota Prius, in the seventy-mile-per-hour freeway zone. This common act has become standard driving procedure in Minnesota. The person behind the wheel might be your Aunt Mabel. Or the aged CEO of your company.

» The Zipper Merge is not a rock band but a means of joining two lanes of traffic in the most efficient, quickest way. While it might make you mad when someone drives past you to merge further ahead, don't sweat it. The zipper works.

» Moose like to lick salt off the pavement of the Gunflint Trail. Watch out for them in the winter.

» When the highway department pulls down the gate on the freeway during a snowstorm, it means it is closed. Seriously closed. As in, hypothermia-awaits-beyond-the-gate closed. An innkeeper will happily put you up for the night.

» At 5 PM on the Friday evening before fishing opener, don't be in a hurry to get out of the Twin Cities. There are fifty miles of boat trailers ahead of you.

» Potholes are like deer. Anticipate the second one. Don't swerve.

» Don't wash your car during the January thaw. Or on a warm day in February. Or during the month of April. It will be filthy again within twenty-four hours anyway.

» It is OK to drive slower during the season's first snowfall. It is called getting your winter driving legs. Drive at your normal speed and all the slower drivers will wave at you while your car is towed from the ditch.

» Tailgate a snowplow, and rock salt won't be the only thing you'll be pulling from your teeth. Stay five car lengths back.

» A roundabout is not a gymnastic move but a funny circle of merges and sloped curbs. And yes, it actually works.

» When you are pulling up to a traffic merge during rush hour and there are two lanes and a stoplight ahead, it's not OK to straddle the middle line and repeat, eeny, meeny, miny, moe. It's OK to just pick a lane.

» Don't try to explain the 494–694 beltway or the 35W and 35E phenomenon to new arrivals to the Twin Cities. All of us need a mystery in our lives. Chances are good you'll get it all wrong anyway.

Field Dress a Deer

WITH ABOUT TWO HUNDRED THOUSAND deer killed by hunters every fall in Minnesota, the art of field dressing is still very much alive. But there are scant resources for new hunters to learn how to do it, other than having a good mentor. After interviewing dozens of venison processors over the years, I've learned it's apparent some hunters should improve their skills. Processors say some hunters do their venison an injustice by poorly dressing their deer, thus increasing the odds of E. coli contamination and wasting a perfectly good venison loin.

Field dressing a deer isn't difficult. The two most important things are to field dress soon after the deer is dead and to keep the carcass cool. Outdoor temperatures over fifty degrees quickly spur the growth of meat-spoiling bacteria.

You'll need a sharp, stout knife and rubber gloves. A small, hand-sized saw (made specifically for deer dressing and available at sporting goods stores) or knife with serrated blade is also handy. Don't use your kitchen utensils; they're usually too dull to do a good job.

» Roll the deer onto its back or side. Wearing your gloves, locate where the hard, V-shaped breastbone ends at the top of the rib cage. There is a bit of cartilage here, then a soft spot where the body cavity begins.

» Make a shallow incision into the body cavity, making sure not to cut any organs. Insert two fingers, form a V, and aim your hand toward the rear legs. Place the knife between your fingers and, while lifting the skin, cut the abdominal wall downward to the pelvic area. The farther you go toward the rear legs, the more organs you will encounter that are pressing against the wall. If you are lifting the skin as you cut, you'll avoid cutting the organs. You'll likely experience a release of smelly air from the body cavity. This is normal, but it's the part that makes most newbies gag.

» If it's a buck, while you're in the pelvic area, separate the external reproductive organs. They will be attached to the skin, but don't cut them off completely. If it's a doe, remove the udder, also attached to the skin, in the groin area.

» With outward pressure applied to the rear legs, cut the flesh where the legs meet at the pelvis, being careful not to cut the deer's urethra. Separate the urethra, and then move to the anus. Cut around the anus and separate it and the urethra from the deer. Some hunters elect to tie off the rectum and urethra with a string.

» Return to the upper abdomen area. Straddle animal, facing toward the head. Using your small saw or serrated knife blade, cut the breastbone upward to the neck region. (If you plan to have the animal mounted, you don't want to cut to the neck and destroy the deer's shoulder cape.)

» Reach into the cavity with your knife and free the windpipe and esophagus by cutting the connective tissue. Sever the windpipe high in the neck and remove from body cavity. Hold the ribcage open and cut around the diaphragm close to the rib cage to sever any connective tissue attached to internal organs. Be careful not to cut organs, especially the intestines.

» Split the pelvic bone with your knife or small saw. Remove rectum and urethra from under pelvic bone.

» Roll animal onto its side so the entrails spill out. Remove excess blood from inside body cavity. Prop open cavity with a stick or other instrument; the key is to cool the inside of the cavity as quickly as possible.

» Before you transport the animal, make sure it is properly tagged.

» Hang the deer as soon as possible, making sure to keep the body cavity open and exposed to cool air. If air temperatures are above fifty degrees, pack the cavity with ice.

Build a Birch-Bark Canoe

ERIK "PITCH" SIMULA has known since age five that he wanted to be around canoes. Growing up near Duluth, he dreamed of becoming a wilderness canoe guide, and as a teenager, he began guiding trips into the Boundary Waters Canoe Area Wilderness for Sommer's Canoe Base and the Voyageur Outward Bound School. Along the way, he was drawn to study the construction of wood and canvas canoes and the birch-bark canoes he came across.

"I knew that the birch-bark canoe was the canoe premiere, a masterpiece of history," he says. In 1992 he began building his own birch-bark. It took him five years to complete the nineteen-foot, Ojibwe-style long-nose canoe.

While many bark canoe builders use modern materials and tools, Simula decided to return to traditional canoe-building skills, using only natural raw materials and his own hands. He found Ojibwe elders who taught him traditional methods of finding materials for birch-bark canoes, the canoe's design, and uses.

In 2009 Simula paddled one thousand miles, following fur-trader routes across Minnesota, in a thirteen-foot birch-bark canoe. He builds one birch-bark canoe each summer.

» How did you learn to build bark canoes?

I learned primarily from two Ojibwe master birch-bark canoe builders and mentors. I also learned from master birch-bark canoe builders Ray Boessel, the grandson-in-law of master builder Bill Hafeman, from Bigfork, Minnesota, and Henri Vallaincourt, from Greenville, New Hampshire. John McPhee wrote about Vallaincourt in his book *The Survival of the Bark Canoe*. I studied with master canoe builder Ralph Freese, who runs the Chicagoland Canoe Base store. I also acquired a copy of *The Bark Canoes and Skin Boats of North America*, by Edwin Tappan Adney and Howard I. Chapelle. The Smithsonian Institution published it in 1965, and it is the primary written source of traditional birch-bark canoe building. Master birch-bark canoe builders David and Ernestine Gidmark researched and published many credible stories, techniques, and photos of past Ojibwe master birch-bark canoe builders. I traveled to Peterborough, Ontario, to study at the Canadian Canoe Museum and continued learning by studying birch-bark canoes in museums, casinos, and old lodges.

» Who were your Ojibwe mentors?

I learned by listening to advice from Leech Lake Ojibwe elder John Mitchell and Lac La Croix Ojibwe elder Gilbert Caribou and by studying the surviving birch-bark canoes of Ojibwe master birch-bark canoe builders Earl Nyholm and others now deceased. I also learned aspects of birch-bark harvest and stitching with spruce root from traditional birch-bark basket maker Pete Gagnon of the Grand Portage Ojibwe.

» Describe how the birch bark is harvested and used.

Only the outer bark of the white birch tree is used for the hull. The bark is usually harvested in late June or July; only then does it separate easily from the cambium, or inner bark, of the tree. The canoe hull should come in a single sheet for the length of the canoe. It should be of thick, blemish-free, uniform strength from a very straight, large diameter, healthy, living tree.

» How do you find the right tree?

Finding the right tree for canoe bark is the most challenging and critical part of canoe building. It can take months or years of scouting to find a suitable tree.

There are many, many considerations, tests, and tricks to gather the perfect piece. Once the piece is cut, it must be gently lowered from the tree, cleaned, rolled, transported, stored, trimmed, and handled with great care to prevent molding or cracking. You must keep it out of direct sunlight to prevent edge curling.

» How much does it weigh?

Due to the high moisture content, a large sheet of bottom bark can weigh as much as one hundred pounds when freshly harvested. It will be six feet wide by twenty feet long.

» What other materials do you use?

I use hand-split and hand-carved northern white cedar for gunwales, planks, ribs, headboards, and stems. I'll also use white cedar for light paddles, wild rice flails, and push poles. For pegs and thwarts, I prefer hardwoods such as white, black, or green ash, white or yellow birch, or red or sugar maple. I use black spruce or tamarack roots that are debarked and hand split for lacing the bark together and lashing canoe parts.

» What about a sealant for the seams?

The sealant is made of spruce or pine resin. It is blackened with charcoal, though some eastern tribes omit this step, and tempered with a small amount of bear grease or other rendered animal fat or fish oil. The proper mixture results in a sealant that is not brittle or tacky.

» How is the boat built?

After all the materials are prepared, boat construction begins by laying the bark on the ground and centering a wooden frame on top of it. The frame is used to shape the bottom length and width of the canoe; different-sized frames are used for different-sized boats. The bark is heated with hot water, folded around the building frame, and held vertically by wooden stakes driven into the ground on the outside of the hull. The bark is laced to shape with an awl and spruce roots. The cedar gunwales, the inwales, and the outwales are pegged and lashed to the top edge of the bark. Hardwood thwarts are mortised, pegged, and lashed to the gunwales. Cedar stems are split, bent, lashed, and attached to cedar headboards to construct the end frames and then laced into each end of the bark hull.

» How is the bark hull strengthened?

I use long, thin cedar planks and thick cedar ribs that I bend over my knee after ladling the wood with boiling water. I insert them to strengthen and expand

One of Eric Simula's birch-bark canoes

the hull using only friction to fit them. Cedar gunwale caps are pegged on top of the gunwale.

» AND TO SEAL THE SEAMS?

The pitch is applied to all the inside seams and cracks in the bark below the waterline. The outside seams are also pitched below the waterline. While modern caulking can make a canoe much more watertight for long periods without maintenance, I like to use the traditional, hand-collected, and hand-mixed pitch for sealing the canoes.

» WHAT TOOLS DO YOU USE?

I prefer to use only hand tools. I split out all wooden parts from a tree with mallets, wooden wedges, and a froe. I carve with a draw knife, using a shaving horse vise and crooked knife to produce the finished parts. While it is more time consuming and labor intensive than using modern tools and materials, I find a sense of purity in the beauty of the finished canoe. I believe preserving the knowledge of traditional construction skills very worthwhile.

» How long does it take to build a bark canoe?

It may take up to a thousand hours for me to make a larger canoe. I estimate a fourth of the total time is spent harvesting the materials, another fourth is used for processing the materials, and half of the time in the canoe's construction. Working alone or with my Ojibwe wife, Dawn, and often with apprentices and students, I normally build one new birch-bark canoe each summer.

» What time of year is best for building a canoe?

I primarily build only in the summer, when the temperatures are warm enough to work with the bark and roots. I scout for straight birch and cedar trees year round and often collect pitch in winter by snowshoe and dogsled travel. Carving wooden canoe parts is often done in colder winter months.

» There are different birch-bark canoe styles. Which do you use for your canoes?

Each tribe in northern North America built birch-bark canoes with a distinctive tribal form, or shape. The forms were based on the types of waterways on which they were used, local climates, and intended uses. They were also artistic, highly finished, and often decorated by bark designs or etching. I build canoes of the Lake Superior Ojibwe forms, both the high-ended old form, or Eastern Ojibwe form, and the contemporary long-nose, or Western Ojibwe form. Because I live in the Lake Superior Ojibwe country, I choose to honor the local cultural, time-proven forms. I also find the Ojibwe old form–shaped canoes very seaworthy and the finest looking.

» You've paddled great distances in your bark canoe. What's the key to making it seaworthy?

It's good design and by that I mean an overall fair shape, wide, shallow arch bottom for stability, slight rocker for maneuverability, adequate depth and sheer. It's also good uniform quality materials and good craftsmanship.

» Do you have to reapply the pitch sealant frequently?

The traditional pitch sealant I use is a little understood aspect of the canoe. It's temperamental. While a canoe can be watertight one day, simple changes in temperature and humidity can cause the pitch to crack, letting in water. Repitching the canoe can be a daily occurrence. Each batch of pitch is different, depending on the species, age, and health of the trees and bears. Each batch is often mixed according to the weather or water temperature or by adding more or less bear grease to obtain the proper flexibility. If I'm traveling, I gather pitch at every opportunity and cook it over the fire. It's carried in a "pitch pot" or on "pitch sticks." If you've taken care to protect the hull, you might travel for weeks without a single drop seeping in.

» WHAT'S IT LIKE TO PADDLE A BIRCH-BARK CANOE?

For me, paddling a bark canoe is surreal. The irregular, extremely buoyant bark hull, native to the land, glides easily across the water, sending natural vibrations which resound harmoniously, creating, if one is aware and focused, a metaphysical portal to spiritual connectivity with the boreal landscape, enlightening and empowering paddler and wildlife alike. It is not cold and tinny sounding like an aluminum canoe. It's more of a unique individual than even a wood canvas canoe. It never leaves unnatural scrape marks on the rocks. A nicely built birch-bark canoe is pleasing to the eye and ear, feels soft and smooth yet firm, and pleasantly smells of cedar. Its natural colors blend with the forest. It is lighter than most canoes to carry. It can be built and repaired in the wilderness by hand. It can last a lifetime or more if cared for well. It is completely biodegradable.

» WHAT INSPIRES YOU TO BUILD BIRCH-BARK CANOES?

My inspiration comes from the birch-bark canoe's artistry, incredible beauty, history, and utility. My passion for life comes from the natural beauty of the land and of creation: the forest, the horizon, the sky, the wildlife, the lakes and rivers, the sounds of the wind, the smell of the air, the sting of winter's deep cold, the warmth of a wood fire. I've always identified with traditional (pre-European contact) indigenous cultural ways and crafts. Also, as a Finnish American, I found it natural to live in the boreal forest and inland lake country. Because I was born and raised in northeast Minnesota, I sought to learn the ways of those who lived on this landscape in the past. It is important to pass on these endangered skills and ethics to future generations, for our peaceful quality of life and so they are not lost forever.

Cooking a Venison Roast

VENISON HAS BEEN a staple all my life. My mother, who grew up in a German-Scottish family, spent her childhood on a dairy farm in northern Minnesota. Despite the abundance of beef on the farm, dairy cows were mostly too valuable to butcher for family consumption, so her father and brothers each fall would shoot several white-tailed deer for the freezer. My mother remembers many meals of venison steak fried in Crisco, served with potatoes and gravy. On my father's side of the family, my grandmother was of Finnish and Norwegian heritage, and I remember her canning venison meatballs and similarly frying venison in Crisco. I was never terribly fond of venison meatballs or fried venison steak, so as an adult who loves hunting deer, I've spent considerable time cooking venison using modern recipes or adapting old recipes with new ingredients. Since fresh herbs are abundant in grocery stores today, it makes sense to use them in venison dishes as well.

The problem with venison (but also its health benefit) is it is extremely lean. Cooking a venison roast highlights this issue because roasting involves exposing the meat to lots of heat for a long period. Not being naturally marbled with fat, a venison roast can get dry in a hurry. Older cookbooks solved this problem by larding the roast, which involves a large larding needle, string, and strips of pork fat. The needle is inserted into roast and, with the attached string, used to pull a strip of pork fat into the roast, a kind of artificial marbling method. In his 1958 book, *Game Cookery in America and Europe*, Raymond R. Camp advises larding for his recipe "Roast Haunch of Venison, Bluhnbach."

"With ¼ pound of salt pork cut into ¼-inch strips, use larding needle to thoroughly lard the haunch," he writes. I've tried larding this way, and it's difficult, time-consuming, and not conducive to a busy, modern lifestyle.

A quicker and easier method to larding is butterflying the roast and placing strips of cooked bacon between the ridges of the roast, and then rolling the roast back together and tying it with kitchen string. Once I tried it, I realized you could introduce other flavors into the interior roast, especially fresh herbs. While some purists might cringe at butterflying a whole venison roast, the method produces roast with a moist, savory flavor and interior.

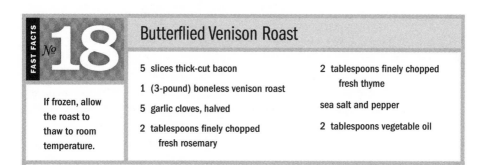

FAST FACTS

№ **18**

Butterflied Venison Roast

If frozen, allow the roast to thaw to room temperature.

5 slices thick-cut bacon

1 (3-pound) boneless venison roast

5 garlic cloves, halved

2 tablespoons finely chopped
    fresh rosemary

2 tablespoons finely chopped
    fresh thyme

sea salt and pepper

2 tablespoons vegetable oil

Cook bacon until soft but not crispy, and set aside. Save bacon fat for searing roast.

Use a sharp knife and begin separating the roast into equal portions by making five to six cuts, but do not cut all the way through the roast. When butterflied, the roast will lay flat on the cutting board in a series of connected ridges of meat. The connected portions should be 1 to 2 inches thick. Take a paring knife and made small incisions into the thickest portions of the roast and insert halved garlic cloves, making sure the cloves are well distributed throughout the roast. Lay cooked bacon strips equal distances apart in crevasses of the butterflied roast. Sprinkle fresh minced herbs over the meat. Do the same with sea salt and pepper.

Roll the roast together again and truss tightly with three lengths of kitchen twine. Place the roast in a hot skillet with the rendered bacon fat and sear the outside until well browned, 10 to 12 minutes, turning with tongs to sear all sides. Coat the outside of the roast with oil. Place roast in a roasting pan on a wire roasting rack, and set in oven preheated to 450 degrees. Cook for 70 to 80 minutes, until internal temperature reaches 125 degrees on a meat thermometer for rare and 130 degrees for medium. Take roast out of oven, tent with aluminum foil, and let stand for 20 minutes. Cut crosswise into 1/4-inch slices and serve with chutney or cherry sauce.

The Essentials of Layering

THE CONCEPT OF LAYERING CLOTHING as a defense against the cold is hardly new, though modern marketing campaigns would lead us to believe it is a fresh concept. Some might mistakenly think the idea is to pile on clothes until you're warm, but that doesn't take into account that the active human body at work produces a lot of heat, which in turn generates sweat.

If you're unable to manage body heat and sweat, and you become sweaty and hot, your body will naturally become cold and clammy. In a worst-case scenario, which plays out frequently among those unfortunate souls lost in the wilderness, the combination of sweaty, wet clothing and cold leads to hypothermia and death.

But let's assume you're not lost and you simply want to stay warm while exerting yourself skiing, canoeing, running, or kayaking. The modern concept of layering focuses on three layers of clothing: the inner layer closest to your skin that wicks away moisture; a middle layer that provides insulation and warmth; and an outer layer, or shell, that blocks wind or moisture, such as rain. Ideally, the outer layer is also breathable, thus moving your body's excess heat away and preventing sweat.

Of course, the concept of layering is perfectly suited to Minnesota's climate, and not just for winter activities. I find myself using the three-layer system in spring and fall, whether I'm running, cutting firewood, or canoeing. There are even cool summer days on the water when I layer, especially if I'm canoeing or kayaking and it's windy. So layering is appropriate no matter the season.

To get a scope of the layering philosophy, I pulled from my library a number of outdoor books on cross-country skiing, sea kayaking, winter camping, ruffed grouse hunting, and canoeing. All cited the benefits of layering for those activities, some as far back as the mid-1980s. Some devote entire chapters to layering.

Curious for a historical perspective, I reviewed Eric Sevareid's 1935 book, *Canoeing with the Cree*, about his and Walter Port's expedition from Minneapolis to Hudson Bay. In Sevareid's equipment list, he includes "heavy wool underwear" and a "heavy sweater apiece" and "four wool blankets rolled in two rubber ponchos." A rubber poncho back then definitely did not breathe like today's modern shell jackets, but Sevareid's use of wool was no doubt an effective layering system. Ironically, the modern outdoor equipment industry has just "rediscovered" wool, with the widespread popularity of merino wool blends for performance underwear and sweaters. Wool is back, in layers.

Garrett and Alexandra Conover, two of North America's modern experts on winter camping, tout the benefits of wool for inner and middle layers and breathable cotton anoraks as a top layer. They are not fans of Gore-Tex as a top layer for cold-weather wear.

"Gore-Tex, nylon and coated nylon all stop wind admirably, but none are breathable in a practical sense," they write in their seminal winter-camping book, *The Winter Wilderness Companion*. They complain that Gore-Tex, for example, will still build up frost inside a jacket shell. Then again, the Conovers spend weeks and months at a time in subzero temperatures in the Canadian bush, whereas a spin around Lake Harriet on cross-country skis won't expose the user of a Gore-Tex shell jacket to the same prolonged harsh elements.

Merino wool, named after its namesake sheep that bears exceptionally fine and soft fibers, is an excellent material for base layer underwear. It wicks moisture, is remarkably odor-free, and isn't itchy like wool used in yesteryear's underwear. Other polyester-spun and microfiber fabrics are good base layers, too, and perhaps ideal for cool and moderate temperatures, but today's wool and wool blends appear to be gaining on modern polyester as a cold-weather first layer.

Wool and fleece are excellent middle layer materials. Fleece vests are comfortable and stylish enough that they're often seen in office environments. On winter camping trips and during the deer hunting season, I rotate between several heavy wool shirts or fleece zippered jackets that become my winter recreation mid-layer. Their ability to provide warmth and breathable wind protection means I sometimes wear them without a top layer.

For wind and rain protection, I'll use a Gore-Tex shell, but I agree with the Conovers that Gore-Tex isn't great for extreme, cold weather. My Gore-Tex shell is great for canoeing and fishing in the rain and walking around the park, but it's not my choice for backcountry skiing, when I'll wear a wool or cotton shell for breathability. However, synthetic shell makers have made up for some of this lack of breathability by adding zippers in the armpit area and other zipped vents.

A well-layered clothing ensemble works best if you're moderately to heavily involved in exercise. Layering still works if you're at an outdoor football game or watching the St. Paul Winter Carnival parade, but here you'll want more insulation if your body isn't generating loads of heat. In those cases, a good down parka as an outer layer can't be beat.

№ **19**

Three Essential Knots

THE TRUCKER'S OR TRAVELER'S HITCH

This combination of a knot and a hitch is very handy for securing loads to a vehicle rooftop or to a trailer. I use it every time I tie a canoe or duck boat on the top of my truck. In the picture-heavy (and helpful) book *Paddle Your Own Canoe*, by Gary and Joanie McGuffin, the McGuffins call it the Traveler's Hitch. Other references I've found call it the Trucker's Hitch, though it seems to have many variations. The knot combination creates a mechanical advantage so you can tighten and secure a load.

Let's say you have a canoe on the roof rack of your vehicle. Tie one end of your rope to one end of the roof rack and toss the remaining rope over the canoe.

Reach up to the portion of the rope lying on the canoe, gather a loop, and make an overhand knot above the loop. Tighten the knot, making sure to keep the loop intact.

Take the tag end of the rope, run it under the rack, and put it through the loop in your rope. You've created a kind of block and tackle. Holding the tag end, cinch the rope and canoe down and tie off with several overhand knots.

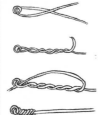

CLINCH KNOT

This knot is a universal and easy method for tying a hook to your fishing line.

Pass the end of the fishing line through the eye of the hook. Keep a small loop in front of the eye.

Twist the tag end of the line around the standing end of the fishing line five times. Pass the tag end through the loop near the eye. Tighten the knot by pulling the hook and the fishing line. Wet the knot with a bit of saliva. Trim tag end close to the hook.

BLOOD KNOT

This is a handy knot for joining two pieces of fishing line or cord together.

Lay side by side two sections of the lines.

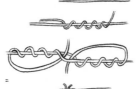

Wrap the tag end of one line around the standing line of the other five times. Pass the tag end of the line back between a center loop created by the two wrapped lines.

Wrap the tag end of the other line around the opposite standing. Pass that tag end through the same loop as the first tag end.

Pull the standing lines tightly to create the knot. Trim the tag ends.

Snowshoeing for Beginners

THERE IS SOMETHING ROMANTIC about the notion of snowshoeing. Perhaps it is the scene of the lonely traveler, steam blowing from the nostrils as the snowshoer effortlessly shuffles across a snowy plain toward a warm, awaiting cabin. After snowshoeing through some very rugged terrain in northern Minnesota, I've shaken that vision of snowshoeing. It's hard work. If you're out of shape or unaccustomed to having snowshoes on your feet, the act of snowshoeing is frustrating and tiring. Your legs soon feel leaden and weak. It's important to note that the alternative—wading through deep snow—is far more tiring.

I've used snowshoes to climb backcountry hills while pulling a pulk, or winter sled, with my gear. I've also used them to cross deep snowfields. In both cases, my backcountry skis were rendered useless by the terrain or the snow depth. Snowshoeing is a faster and easier alternative than using skis, and in all cases I've been grateful to use snowshoes.

There is also a new snowshoe sport today, and it involves running or fast walking on hard-packed trails. There are snowshoe races where very fit people cover rugged courses on packed snowy trails faster than they could in plain running shoes.

In both activities—the backcountry travel and the trail running—the snowshoe serves a vital function: staying afloat on a layer of snow. The alternative would be something called "post-holing," where each leg breaks though the surface and you're left wallowing in ankle-deep or even thigh-deep snow. Snowshoes are an old and time-tested method of snow travel when other means don't work.

Tips for Using Snowshoes

Make sure bindings are in good repair and fit your boot well. It's helpful to test the bindings indoors on a hard surface before taking them outside. Also, it's easier to learn how bindings work and measure them to your boot inside rather than outdoors, where cold weather makes the binding material stiff.

Snowshoeing requires you to step with your feet apart and to lift one shoe over the other. It takes practice, and you're guaranteed to have sore muscles after your first attempt. But stick with it: before too long, you'll find you can pick up speed and maneuver around objects.

It is easier to use snowshoes on a packed surface than on deep, fluffy snow, so it's helpful to practice on the former rather than the latter. Be sure to test your snowshoes in a variety of snow conditions before you take them on an expedition.

Ski poles come in handy to keep you steady and to provide extra leverage. I usually use ski poles on winter camping trips when snowshoes are necessary because the extra help saves my legs, especially when going uphill.

Snowshoes with aluminum claws are handy on sloped and icy hills. However, they may not be necessary or practical on flat surfaces in deep snow.

FAST FACTS № 20 Types of Snowshoes

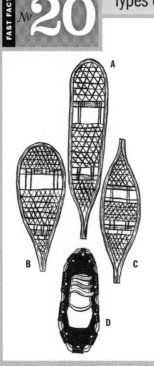

ALASKAN OR YUKON (A): Large snowshoes designed for deep snow. They work well for large people or anyone carrying a large, heavy pack.

MICHIGAN OR MAINE (B): Medium-sized snowshoes with tails that help balance them in deep snow.

OJIBWE (C): Two pointed ends allow them to more easily get through brush and low trees without getting snagged.

METAL HIKERS AND WALKERS (D): Modern metal frames, usually aluminum, are covered with plastic or vinyl. They come in several sizes and have many practical uses, mainly on packed trails. Not useful in deep snow unless the large size is used.

BEARPAW: Wide, oval snowshoes designed to maneuver through trees. Their small size makes them more suitable for small people in shallow snow.

RUNNING SNOWSHOES: Small lightweight snowshoes that don't require the user to spread his or her feet apart.

HILL AND MOUNTAIN SNOWSHOES: Large frames with metal claws or other devices handy for better traction for climbing hills.

Hill climbing in snowshoes is arduous. Try the herringbone step by keeping your feet splayed apart. You can also walk uphill by walking side step or at an angle to the hill.

Be sure to buy snowshoes that will fit your type of travel. I own a pair of wood-framed Maine snowshoes that I use exclusively for backcountry winter camping. They are perfect for this application, and with regular maintenance, they should last most of my lifetime.

Outdoor Adventures for Five-Year-Olds

IF YOU'RE A FIVE-YEAR-OLD Minnesotan, here are ten ways to have fun outdoors:

» Sit on your dad's shoulders and watch the Winter Carnival parade in St. Paul, the Holidazzle parade in Minneapolis, or any small-town Fourth of July parade.

» Get your picture taken while walking across the headwaters of the Mississippi River at Itasca State Park. Catch a fish off the dock in Lake Itasca. Marvel at the giant pine trees in the park.

» Catch bluegills with your grandfather on a northern Minnesota lake or off the dock at your grandparents' cabin. Take a fishing class from the MinnAqua program offered by the Department of Natural Resources.

» Create a collection of rocks from the beaches of Lake Superior. Look for rocks in the shapes of animals or letters of the alphabet. Collect tiny clear or amber-colored rocks and put them in vials or small jars. Expand your collection to other colored rocks.

» Create a terrarium with your parents and fill it with crickets and frogs you find at the lake or in your yard. Release the frogs before fall so they can hibernate outdoors.

» Take a tour of the Minneapolis Sculpture Garden and have your picture taken with the *Spoonbridge and Cherry* sculpture. Go to Franconia Sculpture Park near the St. Croix River and see the very large metal sculptures.

» Go for a bike ride with your parents on the Gateway Trail or along the Mississippi River in the Twin Cities. If your legs aren't long or strong enough to peddle, get your parents to pull you in a trailer.

» Visit the Laura Ingalls Wilder Museum and see the Wilder Pageant in Walnut Grove in southwestern Minnesota. The town is located south and east of Marshall.

» Visit a local farm for pick-your-own raspberries, strawberries, or blueberries. Visit an apple orchard and eat a Honeycrisp apple, a variety developed in Minnesota.

» Visit the Oliver H. Kelley Farm in Elk River and learn how to plow a field with horses or make homemade butter. Visit historic Forestville in Forestville State Park and learn what town life was like in the late 1800s.

How to Back Up a Trailer

WHETHER YOU ARE TOWING a boat or recreation trailer or hauling leaves, knowing how to back up a trailer is an essential skill. It is a confounding act because most of us do it infrequently, and even though I've owned a boat with a trailer most of my adult life, I've experienced the heart-sinking crunch of my trailer hitting some unseen object. Trailer maneuvers can also be a sore spot for couples and friends.

Spend a morning at a busy boat ramp, and eventually you will see the tension. A common scene: one person is driving and the other is giving—or yelling—directions. A couples counselor would have a field day with the frustration and discord.

"Straighten out the wheels!" yells the spotter.

"They are straight!" screams the driver.

You get the idea.

The truth is, anyone who uses a trailer regularly should learn to go solo. Even if you have a spouse or friend who is a loyal partner in recreation or yard work, you may find yourself without your handy spotter someday. Everyone should learn to back up alone.

The key is learning the mechanics of steering the trailer and the effective use of your rearview mirrors. Once you get the hang of that, you'll know how to back up a trailer, and your spotter will not have to yell instructions but only watch for obstacles.

A first step is setting your mirrors for the best view of obstacles behind your trailer. Before backing up, spend a moment adjusting the outside side mirrors and the inside one attached to your windshield. Make sure they give you an optimal view of the trailer and anything else that is immediately to the left and right of your rear bumper. If you own a pickup with a topper, it helps to drop the tailgate and open the rear window or door on the topper to get the best view of your trailer.

The second step is lining up your vehicle and trailer for a straight path to your destination. This is extra time well spent. Pull forward and align your vehicle and trailer for the straightest possible route.

Because the trailer and vehicle are joined, the hitch creates a pivot point between the two. That pivot point causes the trailer to turn in the opposite direction from the vehicle when you back up. This is an important point in understanding how to turn the vehicle's steering wheel. If your hand is at the top of the steering wheel and you turn left while backing up, your vehicle will veer left, but the trailer will go right because of the pivot point at the hitch. So remember: turn right and trailer goes left; turn left and the trailer goes right. Back up slowly, making small adjustments in steering to keep your vehicle and trailer going straight. I sometimes open the driver's door and look back to make a good assessment of my progress.

As you are backing up, try picking a target spot between you and your destination. Try hitting the target spot first, then stop and assess. If you don't have the correct angle to go farther, pull forward slightly, straighten the vehicle and trailer, and try again. Remember to go slowly. If you panic and step on the accelerator, the vehicle and trailer can quickly jackknife.

Practice before you get into a high-tension situation. Take the vehicle and trailer to an empty parking lot and practice until you have a good feel for how the vehicle and trailer interplay while backing up.

Judging Ice Thickness

AROUND LATE NOVEMBER in the Upper Midwest, a strong urge begins tugging at the souls of those who ice skate, play hockey, ice fish, and sail improbable boats with metal runners. They're pulled to the ice that has started forming on lakes and ponds, and when their ice shanties, ice sailing boats, and hockey rinks begin appearing on water bodies, a different segment of a population that clings to terra firma shakes its collective head and cries out, "They're crazy."

Call it the ice counterculture. It's a yin and yang thing—there are people who are drawn to ice, and there are those who shun and distrust it. The truth is, ice is a fairly strong substance capable of holding up semitrucks if thick enough (recall the television show *Ice Road Truckers*), but it is unpredictable and subject to unseen elements such as wind and currents. The Department of Natural Resources is fond of saying, "No ice is 100 percent safe."

FAST FACTS

№ **21**

When Is Ice Safe to Travel On?

Here are guidelines for ice thickness and the weight it can support:

TWO INCHES OR LESS: Stay off. It's too thin to hold up a human, even a child. Keep pets away as well.

FOUR INCHES: Safe for foot traffic. This is when Minnesota's legions of ice anglers begin drilling holes and searching for crappies, walleyes, and northern pike.

FIVE INCHES: Now you can drive a snowmobile or all-terrain vehicle on the ice.

EIGHT TO TWELVE INCHES: Believe it—cars and small trucks can drive on it. On Lake of the Woods, resorters use a small fleet of sub-compact Suzukis, Jeeps, and other small vehicles to ferry anglers to fish houses early in the ice-fishing season, before they begin using larger, tracked vehicles.

TWELVE TO FIFTEEN INCHES: Medium-sized trucks can travel on ice.

MORE THAN FIFTEEN INCHES: It is now safe for large trucks and trailers.

How do you find out how thick the ice is? Check at a local resort or bait and tackle store, whose owners often check ice conditions daily. If you venture on the ice, bring along an ice chisel (also called an ice spud) that is used to chip small holes for testing. A tape measure or ruler comes in handy for slipping into the hole and checking thickness. Ice anglers use motorized ice augers that can quickly drill holes to see how thick the ice is.

Never assume ice is the same thickness across a water body. Springs, rotting vegetation, or currents can create thin spots and even open water. Wind can create dramatic changes to ice. Anglers have sometimes been caught on ice floes on large lakes when winds push ice and create cracks or gaps of open water.

Ice picks are important safety devices for ice travelers. They are wooden pegs with a sharp nail embedded at one end. If you fall through the ice, you can use the picks to pull yourself to safety.

Paint a Winning Waterfowl Stamp

JOE HAUTMAN AND HIS BROTHERS, Jim and Bob, never went to art school, but they're considered among the most skilled and best waterfowl artists in the country. Between them, they have won ten federal duck stamp contests, an unprecedented family streak for the competition that raises money for wetland conservation through stamp sales. The brothers were raised in St. Louis Park in a family of seven children, and they were inspired by their parents in different ways: their mother is a painter and their late father was an avid waterfowl hunter who collected waterfowl stamps. He was also an erstwhile painter, and Joe has one of his waterfowl paintings in his home.

The Hautman brothers were immortalized in a brief scene in the movie *Fargo*, when Marge Gunderson's artist husband complains about his chances of winning a duck stamp contest because "the Hautmans" have entered it, too. The name cameo wasn't a coincidence: the Hautmans grew up on the same street as *Fargo* directors Ethan and Joel Coen. The artists also donated props for the movie.

Migratory Bird Hunting and Conservation Stamp

U.S. Department of the Interior

Void after
June 30, 2009

$15

Northern Pintails

The 2008–9 federal duck stamp, art by Joe Hautman

Joe is a four-time winner of the federal duck stamp contest (2011, 2007, 2001, and 1991). Jim has also won four times, and Bob twice. While Joe has a doctorate and a master's degree in physics from the University of Michigan, he decided to leave his career in academia after he won his first federal stamp contest.

» ON METHOD.

Hautman is modest when it comes to describing his painting methods. In fact, he doesn't really have one. "I don't have any secrets when it comes to method," Hautman says. "It's related to the reason I wasn't too into teaching in my science career. Even in science, I never had a method." Hautman says he thinks in terms of pictures. When asked for driving directions to Minneapolis's Uptown, for example, he instantly forms a picture in his mind of all the various routes and is likely to offer several different answers to the question. "It can be confusing for people," he says. "I've never had much technique, and I never do two paintings in the same way. I wouldn't make a good teacher."

Sometimes he will start a painting by doing the background first; sometimes the animal is first (he's well known for his jungle and songbird scenes, too). For duck stamps, the emphasis must be on the bird and less on its background, so Hautman spends a lot of time making his backgrounds as simple as possible.

He typically paints with acrylics but has experimented with other mediums, even colored pencils. He said acrylics work well because they dry fast. "It takes so long for oil paint to dry, and I'm always finishing at the last minute," he says.

» ON USING PHOTOS.

Hautman uses photos to help him capture details of a duck. "In an ideal world, I would have the perfect photograph, and I would copy that photograph, but it never happens that way. Normally I might use fifty to a hundred photographs. On the last federal stamp that I won, it was a wood duck, and the design was inspired by a particular photograph that I had taken five years earlier. It had an attitude that I liked. Though I ended up putting on a different head and different eye, I was always trying to preserve the attitude that was captured in the original photo."

» ON WORK HABITS.

On average, Hautman paints about ten works a year, spending a bit more than a month on each, though each painting varies in time with its complexity. He is not a night owl. "I probably work better in the morning," he says. "I can work at night, but the thing I notice working at night is things take longer. I'm not as effective at night. There is a lot of tedious stuff with painting, and I'll leave that kind of stuff to working at night." Focusing is never a problem. Sometimes Hautman gets lost in a project, spending hours without leaving his easel. "I can sit down and paint for ten hours," he says. "Focused, yes, but on the blue chips things? Maybe not. I could be focusing on something that is ultimately going to be covered up by the frame. I love the process of painting. I'm not real goal oriented. I'm more process oriented."

» ON CRITIQUES.

The Hautman brothers are famously known for critiquing each other's work. They find it enormously helpful, and each welcomes critiques from the others. "It's an important part of our process, definitely," says Joe. Don't expect him to discuss how a painting might reveal his inner self, though. "Some people talk about that, but I don't want that," he says. "I sort of want to get rid of my individual stamp on a painting."

» ON PAINTING FOR OTHERS.

Painters have worked for kings, popes, and governments big and small. Hautman takes a similar view of his paintings—they're not for his enjoyment, but for others. "I think of painting as something you do for other people," he says. "By the time I'm done with a painting, I'm sick of it. I'm not painting to have something that turns me on. It's for others to enjoy."

» ON PAINTING UNDER PRESSURE.

Hautman admits to being a terrible procrastinator, sometimes finishing a water-fowl stamp painting on the day it's due. "I'm not that extreme anymore," Joe says. "I've even sent it a day early the last few times. Deadlines, I have to admit, are good for me."

Crop Art 101

VISIT THE AGRICULTURAL BUILDING at the Minnesota State Fair, and you will inevitably be drawn to the crop art exhibit. Maybe it is because of the art form's uniqueness or the talent of the artists, but visiting the crop art exhibit has become a touchstone experience at the state fair. The art form was certainly elevated by the late Lillian Colton, the grand dame of crop art, whose work has been displayed in fine-art museums and who was featured many times on late-night television shows before her death at age ninety-five in 2007.

Liz Schreiber of Minneapolis is a crop art artist, aficionada, and regular exhibitor at the state fair. Her portrait of Vincent Price was the 2006 amateur division winner in the natural color category.

» HOW DID YOU GET INTO SEED ART?

It was all about the state fair. I moved to Minnesota in 1995 to go to graduate school. I have a very good friend who introduced me to the state fair, and it was always high on the list of things for us to see. Crop art was always one of my favorite parts of the fair. I admired it and decided I wanted to try doing it myself. I have a fine arts background, and it's not completely foreign to me to put together images. I did my first crop art piece in 2004.

» DID YOU HAVE A CROP ART MENTOR?

No. I discovered www.cropart.com, which got me started on how to look for seeds and learn about the state fair rules and regulations, of which there are many. I did my own research and went at it. Alan Carpenter did a triptych that made a big impression on me. It features Lawrence Welk, the Corn Palace, and Myron Floren. It's really spectacular.

» DESCRIBE YOUR ART BACKGROUND.

I studied sculpture and print making in undergraduate school in Richmond, Virginia. I worked several years as a glass blower, and during that time, I decided to go back to school and study costume design. I decided to move to Minnesota and study theater arts. I worked at the Guthrie for several years as a scenic painter. I work today as a freelancer, painting scenes for commercials, theater, advertising, and photography sets.

» WHEN YOU TELL PEOPLE YOU DO CROP ART, WHAT'S THEIR REACTION?

People who know what it is get really excited. A lot of people see my work at the state fair and say, "Oh my god, you made that?" They ask a lot of questions like where do you buy your seeds. There is always a lot of interest in the details. Then there are people who don't know what the hell crop art is.

» WHERE DO YOU GET YOUR SEEDS?

A variety of places. At the food co-op in the bulk section. I love going to the bulk section where there are these clear tubes of beans, seeds, and rices. It's like a paint palette. Farm co-ops, but they usually sell their seeds in fifty- to hundred-pound bags. They've been kind enough to open them up and let me look at them. Even the grocery store has new and interesting things. Any time I go to an Asian or Indian grocery, I check out their edible seeds and beans.

» CAN YOU SHARE WHAT SEEDS YOU USE?

It's no secret. There are a couple different millets. Poppy seeds, corn, peas, lentils, several types of clovers. Flax. Quinoa. Wild rice. I've used amaranth, kidney, pinto, and azuki beans. Canola seed. Buckwheat groats. Thistle. Mustard seed. There are all kinds of grasses, of course, that are usable.

» DOES SEED SIZE MATTER?

When I first started, I was still learning what was out there. My earlier stuff has

Liz Schreiber's *Colonel Sanders*, 2007

bigger seeds. As I get more involved, I try to find smaller stuff for more detail and intricacy.

» WHAT KIND OF GLUE DO YOU USE?

Just plain Elmer's white glue.

» WHAT ARE YOUR SIGNATURE DESIGNS?

I do portraits of people. I like to include a decorative frame made from seeds as part of the piece. I've done Slim Whitman, Colonel Sanders, Frankenstein, Bo Diddley. It's usually someone who has inspired me. Evel Knievel.

» YOU WERE INSPIRED BY COLONEL SANDERS?

I'm not such a big fried-chicken eater, but he's got such a good look. He's an American icon. There is a kind of cheeseballness that I'm attracted to.

» HOW LONG DOES IT TAKE?

It depends on the size of the portrait. I'd say like a month for a larger piece; for a smaller piece, maybe a couple of weeks.

» DO YOU PAINT THE IMAGE FIRST?

I usually find an image I like, but I like to translate it and make it my own. I'll do an underpainting first before adding seeds. It's crucial to have something to work from.

» HOW DO YOU DECIDE WHERE CERTAIN SEEDS GO?

It's more impromptu. I know if I'm doing flesh tones, I'll use this seed or that. But if it comes to what someone is wearing or other details, I'll play around with it. I'll lay out stuff and look at it and experiment with it. I'll do an outline and see what different seeds look like in a certain area of texture. The background is the last thing I do.

» ARE FACIAL FEATURES HARD?

When you do somebody's eyes, it's a matter of the tiniest movement of one direction of a seed to get it right. I like to start with the eyes. If I can get the eyes right, the rest can fall into place. You can see a person's character in the eyes.

» ARE THERE CERTAIN SEEDS THAT MAKE GOOD FACIAL FEATURES?

It depends on what you're going for. I've seen great pieces made with all giant seeds. But for what I like to do—it's more realistic and less stylized—I'd say the smaller seeds you can get, the more nuanced you can get with shading. With a paintbrush, you can blend colors. It's not exactly the same with seeds, but you can layer stuff to get the same effect.

» Do you ever have to start over?

I wouldn't start over completely, but I have had things I've taken off and redone.

» Is crop art high art?

I think it is. I know Lillian Colton had a show at the Minneapolis Institute of Arts; that's the only time I've heard of crop art in a museum. I did a couple of demos at the Walker and at the Minneapolis Institute. I know people associate kitschiness with it. That's what attracted me to it. The more I've done it, the more I feel like I'd like to explore it as a fine art.

» How should novices get started in crop art?

www.cropart.com is really fantastic and a good start. I would suggest they go to their food co-op and grocery store and look at the different colors. If there is an image they are thinking of creating, they can think of color and texture. Go see some crop art in person. When I teach crop art, I try to impart that it doesn't have to be super realistic. It can be abstract. The fun is doing it, not necessarily worrying about the finished product. The material is readily available and cheap: glue, beans, and seeds. It's pretty accessible.

» How about the state fair?

If you're interested in entering something at the state fair, read the rules on their website. There are a lot of different categories, and it might affect how you go about it. It's a lot of fun to enter things at the state fair. It's a great way to start.

Dog Mushing: Understanding the Dogs and the Musher

DAVE FREEMAN GREW UP in Illinois but found his love of the outdoors in the Boundary Waters. When he hasn't been guiding canoe trips in the wilderness, he has circumnavigated Lake Superior in a kayak, canoed the length of the Amazon River, and paddled a kayak from Seattle to Alaska. Since 1999 he has guided dogsled trips in the Boundary Waters for Wintergreen Dogsled Lodge. When he and his wife, Amy, were married on White Iron Lake in Ely, guests were ferried across the lake on eight dogsled teams. He and Amy spent a winter dogsledding across Canada's

Northwest Territories, covering nine hundred miles through some of the most remote territory in North America. Their eleven-thousand-mile, multiyear expedition across North America by foot, canoe, kayak, and dogsled is called North American Odyssey. It is followed by thousands of schoolchildren though the couple's website and educational programs.

» HOW DO YOU GET A SLED TEAM READY IN THE MORNING?

We'll go down and give them small amounts of food and water. We try to give them a while to digest, and we'll have breakfast inside the lodge, and then we go down and harness the dogs. We put the harness on each dog, connect each to the sled on the gang line, and once everybody is hooked up, then we take off.

» AT WINTERGREEN, HOW MANY MILES DO YOU GO IN A TRIP?

We generally go about fifteen miles a day and, on average, five days a week, so it is about seventy-five to one hundred miles a week.

» DESCRIBE YOUR NORTHWEST TERRITORIES TRIP.

We spent two and a half months on the trail, going through a series of very remote communities. We had four people—Amy and I and another couple—and twelve dogs. We would take turns: two people would mush each day, and two people would be on skis. The dogs would pull the camping gear and other goods, and if the conditions were good, the musher would stand on the sled.

» HOW MANY MILES A DAY WOULD YOU GO?

It depended on conditions. Some days we covered thirty miles; other days we would cover just ten miles. It really depends on the depth of snow, temperature, and daylight. It was generally slow travel, on unbroken trails. We would encounter snowmobile trails at times and winter roads where we could travel faster.

» WHAT DO SLED DOGS EAT?

Mushers use a high-energy dog food made for working dogs that is high in protein and fat. There are many different brands. Oftentimes, meat is used as well, especially during races when the dogs are really working hard. You can provide them ground-up chicken or beef, mixing that with water. It helps to get them to drink and gives a boost of protein.

» WHEN YOU TRAVEL IN CANADA, DO YOU FEED THEM THE SAME?

In the Northwest Territories, we feed each one high-energy dog food, about two pounds, and a quarter pound of lard. When it's really cold, the beef provides good, extra calories. Sometimes if we caught a lake trout through the ice, we would give

№ 22   Mushing Terms

Dave Freeman and the dogs on the Mackenzie River in the Northwest Territories

LEAD DOG: The first dog on a team, the lead dog is picked for its intelligence, experience, and relationship with the musher. Lead dogs aren't usually the strongest or biggest dog.

WHEEL DOG: Typically a big, strong dog placed directly in front of the sled to provide maximum pulling and some maneuvering skills.

TEAM DOGS: The pair of dogs in the back half of the team and directly in front of the wheel dogs.

GANG LINE: A long rope or cable connected to the sled that stretches the length of the dog team. Each dog is connected to the gang line.

TUG LINE: Rope or cable that connects dogs to the gang line.

NECK LINE: Rope or cable that connects the dogs' collars to the gang line.

SNOW HOOK: A large metal hook, connected to the gang line, which the musher pushes into the ground at every stop. The mushing version of a parking brake, it keeps the team from moving forward.

BRAKE: A hinged metal tool located at the rear of the sled. The musher stands on it to brake.

GEE: Command to turn right, said with a soft "g."

HAW: Command to turn left.

HIKE: Command for dogs to start pulling sled from a stopped position.

WHOA!: Stop. Musher applies brake when making whoa command.

them some fish. On other long trips, I've fed dogs almost exclusively fish. That's a traditional diet for many native people in Canada to feed dogs.

» DESCRIBE A MUSHER'S RELATIONSHIP WITH DOGS.

Sled dogs have an innate desire to run. The main thing is developing a strong bond between the musher and the dogs. The musher has to really know the dogs, so the dogs can trust the musher and understand the musher.

» IS THERE A PACK MENTALITY WITH SLED DOGS?

Definitely, especially the dogs I'm used to working with, which are Canadian Inuit dogs. They're big, freight dogs. There is a hierarchy among them, like a wolf pack. Understanding that hierarchy is important. A team will have boss dogs; they are more dominant over other dogs. They are generally not the lead dogs, but the lead dog and boss dog can play a role in leading.

» DOES IT MATTER WHERE DOGS ARE PLACED ALONG THE GANG LINE?

That's probably the biggest challenge with dogsledding—getting to know the dogs and figuring out where they will perform the best and who they will run well next to. Some dogs will run really well next to another dog, but if they run behind that dog, they might not do well. Their placement in the team is important, and it doesn't always stay the same. Since they can't talk to you, you have to understand body language and visual clues about what makes them happy, scared, frustrated, and what is fun for them.

» HOW DO YOU CHOOSE A GOOD LEAD DOG?

It's a training process. For certain dogs, when you start running them, they may seem to show an interest in leading. When you call a command, maybe their ears perk up. You can move those dogs farther forward in the team and maybe run them next to an experienced lead dog. It's often easier for a lead dog to learn from another experienced lead dog.

» HOW ABOUT A FAVORITE LEAD DOG?

My favorite lead dog is named Fennel. He's half Huskie and half black Lab, a bit of an accident. He's been a great dog, he was one of our lead dogs last winter, and he's twelve years old. We've been expecting him to retire, and he keeps going and going.

» DESCRIBE A GOOD WHEEL DOG.

The closer the dogs are to the sled, the more weight they will pull. Generally your strongest dogs are back toward the sled. When you go around a corner and the sled is pulled into something like a tree, a good wheel dog will swing wide to pull the sled around it.

» Do you have a favorite wheel dog?

One of my favorite wheel dogs is named Bubba. He is a really strong dog. We took him to a weight pulling competition, and he pulled one thousand pounds and won the competition. He has a good mental attitude and the physical traits to be a good wheel dog. He has that innate desire to pull.

» Is mushing more than a winter job?

A lot of being a successful musher is spending time with the dogs. It's feeding and caring for them year round and spending time running them. It doesn't just happen when there is snow on the ground. A lot of mushers run their dogs in the summer using four-wheelers. The actual dogsledding only happens four months of the year, but the training and dog care is a year-round process.

» What's the most important skill for a musher?

It's being patient and level headed. When you are working with [the dogs], they can be stressful. They are barking and lunging, and if they don't do what you want them to do, it can be frustrating. Being mad or yelling isn't helpful. They generally respond better to positive reinforcement than negative.

» How are you positive?

It's being consistent and firm but encouraging—that's the biggest thing. You can make it so dogs are enjoying their day and that they understand they are doing a good job. Do that, and they will perform well for you.

» What can sled dogs teach us?

To get enjoyment out of the simple things in life. Sled dogs get joy out of pulling the sled, getting affection from people, and having a good meal. They look forward to those things. If you think about it, getting exercise, enjoying our friends and relatives, and having a good meal are the simple things in life that we should enjoy more.

Upland Bird Hunting

Hunting Ruffed Grouse

Ruffed grouse are Minnesota's most popular game bird. Beginning in mid-September and running through January, the ruffed grouse season attracts, on average, more than 110,000 hunters annually. There is a reason. Ruffed grouse are forest birds, and Minnesota has an abundance of forest habitat, much of it in the form of public land open to hunting. The state is among the top three in ruffed grouse harvest, but its abundance of public forests is the main reason Minnesota ranks among the nation's best ruffed grouse–hunting states. The ruffed grouse is also arguably the best tasting of all upland game birds. With the sport's exciting flushes combined with the bird's availability, the ruffed grouse is a premiere bird to hunt.

However, ruffed grouse are everywhere and nowhere in the woods; that is to say, they're widespread in Minnesota forests, but they prefer certain habitats for food and protection from predators. You can walk for hours and never see a bird, but wander into the right habitat, and you'll find covey after covey. It's well documented that ruffed grouse eat many types of vegetation, including clover and fern leaves, small berries, and buds. Their preference for hazel bush and aspen catkins—small buds at the end of branches—is well understood by hunters, and the types of habitats where all these foods are found are where hunters focus their search for grouse.

Perhaps the most common method to hunt grouse is to walk forest roads and trails in the mornings and evenings, preferably in the company of a hunting dog. Along the trails, grouse will feed on clover and fern leaves and any berries or catkins growing nearby. A good pointing bird dog will search out birds and alert the hunter to a bird's presence by going on point, after which the hunter will walk forward and flush the grouse. Hunters using flushing dogs, such as Labradors or spaniels, have to be on their toes because a grouse won't hold long for a snuffling bird dog, but both retrievers and pointers are very handy for finding and retrieving downed grouse as well.

Grouse are famous for inhabiting stands of young aspens that are ten to fifteen years old and the diameter of a man's wrist. This is also very difficult habitat to hunt because the trees grow so densely, a situation that favors the grouse's keen ability to escape. But hunters can have success in these thick vegetative areas if they become quick shots and use a pointing dog.

Hunters, however, search out other habitats with berry bushes, such as dogwood, or forest edges with clumps of alder or hazel. I've fruitlessly hunted young aspen for hours, only to move to another grove of mature aspen that was crowded with hazel bushes and find lots of grouse feeding on the budlike catkins that are about a half inch long and the diameter of a pencil eraser. Sometimes when you find grouse concentrating on certain foods, you'll flush multiple birds in a covey. Coveys are also common early in the hunting season when family groups have yet to break up.

Ruffed grouse are strong erratic flyers, and while you can find them after a first or second flush, they seem to get wilier with each encounter. Hunters tend to use twenty and twelve gauges with small-sized shot. The best skill to have as a grouse hunter is to quickly shoulder your shotgun, find the flying grouse through the trees, and anticipate a killing shot. Some hunters, particularly those who are novices, will take a grouse on the ground, but it's not considered sporting (though most experienced grouse hunters can recall shooting their first grouse off the ground when they were young).

Hunting Ring-Necked Pheasants

Ring-necked pheasants share a few characteristics with ruffed grouse. They have a white-meated breast, are powerful flyers, and can be located based on the foods

FAST FACTS №23	Upland Bird Hunting Facts	
	RUFFED GROUSE	**RING-NECKED PHEASANT**
SEASON	Mid-September through January	Mid-October to early January
FOOD	Clover and fern leaves, small berries, hazel bush and aspen catkins	Waste grains such as corn, wheat, and soybeans
HABITAT	Stands of young aspens	Thick grass in agricultural areas
HUNT WITH	Twenty- and twelve-gauge shotgun with small-sized shot	Twelve- or twenty-gauge shotgun with #2 steel shot
DOGS	Pointing or flushing dogs	Flushing and pointing dogs

Success: pheasant and Labrador

they eat. But that's where the similarities end. The pheasant is a big, gaudy bird that lives on the prairies; the grouse is a bird of the forest. With pheasants, you can only shoot the colorful males, or rooster pheasants; with grouse, the genders are impossible to distinguish on the wing, so it's legal to hunt both. Pheasant populations are stymied by deep snows; ruffed grouse thrive in fluffy, deep snow and actually roost in it for protection. Pheasants in Minnesota exist on the northerly edge of their North American range, which is roughly central and west-central Minnesota; ruffed grouse range ever farther north into Canada. Ruffed grouse are native to Minnesota; pheasants are not. The ring-necked pheasant is an introduced species from China, brought to the United States (specifically Oregon) in the early 1900s, after which they thrived and were introduced to other states in the early twentieth century.

In terms of pure hunting excitement, the ringneck is arguably the more dashing and heart thump–producing bird. Despite its size (it can weigh three pounds), the ringneck can be an elusive bird, choosing either to run or fly to evade a hunter and dog. As in grouse hunting, the successful pheasant hunter must know where birds feed and when. In most cases, pheasants feed on waste grains such as corn, wheat, and soybeans during the day and roost in prairie grass at night. That makes the pheasant a bird of agricultural areas, and most hunts occur near crop fields. Pheasants flush quickly and typically out of gun range when they are caught in open ground, but they will hold for a pointing or flushing dog in thick grass, which is where most pheasants are shot.

Still, an abundance of corn and grass doesn't mean a successful pheasant hunt. A rooster pheasant may run hundreds of yards in the grass, evading a hunting dog close on its tail, or it may sit tight and wait until the hunter has passed. Sometimes rooster pheasants become so wary of hunters that they flush from a field as soon as a hunter shuts the door on his vehicle. This behavior is more typical of pheasants living in heavily pressured public hunting areas toward the end of the season. The pheasant season begins in mid-October and runs to the beginning of January.

Most pheasant hunters prefer the larger twelve-gauge shotgun over a twenty, but many skilled pheasant hunters view a twenty gauge as more sporting. While a great many roosters are shot on public land, most are hunted and killed on private land, given that most lands in agricultural areas are privately owned. The challenge for pheasant hunters is gaining access to private land and knowing where private land boundaries are. Asking permission to hunt private land is mandatory to avoid trespassing violations, but over the years, I've rarely been turned down for permission to hunt unless the land has been reserved for a landowner's relative or friend.

Once winter and snow arrive, pheasants typically retreat to the heaviest cover possible, which in Minnesota is cattail sloughs. Walking through cattails is some of the hardest work an upland bird hunter will encounter; some avoid it all together, but there are pheasant hunters who look forward to the challenge and exertion of cattail hunting. Matted down and woven together, cattails in a frozen slough can be a thigh-burning frustration for hunters, but when a pheasant gets up, it is an exciting place to be with a bird dog and a shotgun.

What It Takes to Be a Fishing Guide

JEFF SUNDIN NEEDED A CAREER CHANGE. It was the early 1980s, and he was an operations manager for a courier company. In his spare time, he could be found casting and trolling for walleyes on Lake Minnetonka and other lakes in the western Twin Cities metro, but the hours and pressures of his job were taking a toll on him—and he hated being in the office.

"You see all five lights blinking on the telephone, and the truck is broken down," he recalls. "You never stopped."

He started guiding anglers on some of his favorite lakes around the metro. He got a business card and began taking clients to northern lakes. He was living in the Twin Cities but listed Cedar Point Resort on North Star Lake as his home base "up north." "That was the only lake up there that I knew how to fish," he says. In 1985 he cut the cord to urban living and moved to Deer River in Itasca County, where a thousand lakes are surrounded by tall pines, deep swamps, and plenty of back roads to explore. His fish guiding service flourished, and he never looked back to city life.

» IF YOU NEEDED JUST A FEW ESSENTIALS TO BE A FISHING GUIDE, WHAT WOULD THEY BE?

Everyone is going to have a different idea about what items are "essential." For me, the equipment is fairly simple, but today I couldn't do my job without a few things. Mechanically, a good fish-locating graph, a reliable boat, engine, and trolling motor, and great fishing rods are all what I'd call required equipment.

» IS THERE SOMETHING MORE THAN EQUIPMENT?

You must possess the desire to please people. You simply cannot survive as a guide unless it pleases you to see other people succeed. Loving to fish and being a good fisherman are not good enough reasons to be a guide.

» SO YOU HAVE TO BE ABLE TO ENTERTAIN PEOPLE?

It's important to entertain. Everybody likes to catch fish, and most of the time it works out. You have to look the guy in the face and find something to talk about right off the bat. You have the whole day to talk.

» WHAT IS A GOOD ICE BREAKER TO START A CONVERSATION WITH A CLIENT?

Everyone has a personality all their own, it takes a little trial and error to figure out where to start, but generally, once I know what a customer is interested in, I can get them to tell me about it. It is sort of like being a talk show host. Everybody is good at something, and most of them are proud of their accomplishments. If I just keep asking questions and let them open up, I will almost always learn more than they do.

» HOW DO YOU HANDLE THE PRESSURE TO CATCH FISH?

I try not to feel pressure. If you're under pressure to catch fish, you can't do it. If the name of the game is to go out and catch fish, you ought to be out there enjoying something else. You can call me crazy, but the fish know if you're uptight. They know if you're trying too hard to catch them and they won't bite.

» WHO IS EASIER TO GUIDE, A SKILLED OR UNSKILLED ANGLER?

When you get people who don't know how to fish, it makes the trip easier. They will listen to your advice. The guy you have to worry about is the one who says, "Don't worry about me. I know what I'm doing."

» DOES BEING A FISHING GUIDE REQUIRE MECHANICAL SKILLS LIKE BOAT REPAIR?

It requires a variety of skills. Since there's no "down time" between trips, I have to know how to make repairs on the fly. I do all of my own boat and equipment rigging, so a working knowledge of wiring, minor mechanical issues, and general nuts and bolts of what makes the rig function is essential. By doing my own rigging, I know how everything was installed, and it simplifies diagnosing problems.

» COULD YOU HAVE MADE A LIVING AS A FISHING GUIDE FIFTY YEARS AGO, BEFORE

TODAY'S TECHNOLOGICAL ADVANCES?

I think I would have been better. The GPS? It's handy. I can't really say I don't love having that. In some ways it's easier today, but I have to force myself to go see the new equipment.

» DO YOU NEED A SIXTH SENSE TO CATCH FISH?

There are fishing guides and then there are fishing guides. There are guides who like the idea of being a fishing guide, but they don't have that sixth sense. There is a group of guides that—it never seems to fail—they'll come in at the end of the day, and you never count them out. People say, "When Joe comes in, Joe will have fish."

» WHAT'S THE HARDEST PART OF YOUR JOB? THOSE RARE DAYS WHEN THE FISH AREN'T BITING?

The hardest single thing is adjusting to weather changes. There's nothing worse than having a great game plan that can't be accomplished because the weather forces a last-minute change. All of the planning in the world is occasionally tossed out the window when conditions force you to change.

» MOST PEOPLE GO FISHING FOR VACATION. WHAT DOES A FISHING GUIDE DO FOR A VACATION?

I go fishing. I just try to do something a little different than what I do every day. Sometimes it's as simple as trying a different lake. Sometimes it means trying a different style, or fishing for an unusual species. My second choice is to work in the garden. There's something really nice about playing in the dirt.

» HAS FISHING LOST ANY OF ITS APPEAL IN THE THREE DECADES THAT YOU'VE DONE IT PROFESSIONALLY?

No; if anything, I just keep getting more curious. Twenty years ago I thought I knew a lot; fifteen years ago I realized that I didn't. Today I feel like I'm running out of time if I want to learn everything that I want to learn.

» HOW HARD WOULD IT BE TODAY TO DO WHAT YOU DID—LEAVE A CAREER AND START A NEW ONE AS A FISHING GUIDE?

The mechanical aspects of fishing are easier now than they were then. I could learn how to catch fish faster today than I could when I started. If you love people and love to please them, then that would be easy, too. Unfortunately, it's a lot more expensive to get started today. Newcomers face the challenge of getting up and running fast enough to keep up with the bills. I had the luxury of building my business slowly. Today I think it would be a much more intense experience.

» WOULD YOU RATHER GUIDE A SINGLE INDIVIDUAL OR A GROUP OF PEOPLE?
One on one or smaller family groups are the best for me. I love how people become friends over time. Relationships with the families tend to develop faster for me because they tend to all have similar interests.

Large groups are fun in their own way, but it's common for everyone in the boat to have different interests. Sometimes when I try to satisfy one of them, I leave another one feeling disappointed. There's not always enough time to meet everyone's expectations on the same trip. Many times it's a "one-shot deal," so I don't get a second chance to make 'em smile.

» WHAT'S THE WORST PART OF DEALING WITH PEOPLE'S EXPECTATIONS?
The hard part is meeting my own expectations. It's common for my customers to be a lot more understanding about a tough day than I am. It's easy to say, but I really do try to put myself in their shoes, and I want them to have the kind of experience that I'd want for myself. People can always tell if you're giving it your best effort, and I try really hard not to let myself coast, even on an easy day.

» WHAT'S THE SKILL THAT HAS MADE YOU GOOD AT WHAT YOU DO?
I have told many customers and lots of friends that I am simply too stubborn to quit.

Cold Weather Fun

» Take a banana outside and watch it freeze. Try pounding nails into a board with it.
» Try blowing soap bubbles from a child's bubble kit. They will freeze into fragile balls resembling Christmas tree ornaments.
» Take boiling water or hot coffee outside and toss a cup of it into the air. It will evaporate into a fog, and little of the liquid will reach the ground. This is one of the most popular extreme-cold-weather experiments, duplicated many times on YouTube.
» Walk out on a frozen lake—making sure that the ice is safe—and listen to the moaning and groaning of the lake ice forming.

» Take a balloon outside and watch it deflate as the warm air inside it contracts. Take it back inside and watch it expand again.

» Try this experiment with children to highlight the different freezing points of liquids. Set out small cups containing dish soap, olive or vegetable oil, water, sugar water, and vinegar. See which one freezes first.

Town Name Pronunciation

Aitken	AAY-kin	Menagha	Muhn-NAH-ga
Anoka	Uh-NO-kuh	Mille Lacs	Mill LACKS
Baudette	Buh-DETT	Minneapolis	Min-ee-AP-poh-lis
Bemidji	Beh-MID-jee	New Prague	New-PRAYG
Chisholm	CHIS-uhm	Nicollet	NIK-oh-let
Cloquet	Kloh-KAY	Osakis	Oh-SAY-kis
Duluth	Duh-LOOTH	Otsego	Aht-SEE-go
Edina	Ee-DIE-nuh	Pequot Lakes	PEE-kwaht
Faribault	FAIR-ih-bow	Ranier	Ruh-NEER
Kabetogama	Ka-buh-TOH-guh-muh	Sebeka	Suh-BEE-kuh
Kandiyohi	Kan-dee-YOH-hy	Shakopee	SHOK-oh-pee
Lac qui Parle	LAK ki-PAR-uhl	Taconite	TAK-uhn-yte
Lake Winnibigoshish		Wabasha	WAH-buh-shaw
	Win-nee-beh-GOSH-ish	Wanamingo	Wahn-uh-MING-goh
Le Sueur	Luh SOOR	Waseca	Wah-SEE-kuh
Lutsen	LOOT-sen	Waskish	WAHS-kish
Mahnomen	Muh-NOH-min	Wayzata	Why-ZET-ah
Mahtomedi	Mah-toh-MEE-dy	Zumbrota	Zuhm-BROH-tuh

Your Trip Up North

WHEN I WAS A KID living not far from a dozen or two resorts in Itasca County, I'd ride to the general store at Voigt's Resort and drink grape pop with my dad. Visiting the lake, casting for walleyes, listening to loons, sitting on the dock—this is what we did most weekends in the summer. I never realized that these activities were once-a-year vacation memories for the city kids I saw at the beach. As an adult, I moved to the Cities and the roles were switched—I was the tourist and not the lake-country resident—and I gained more appreciation for the rhythms and rituals of summer vacation "Up North." Now a new trend has emerged—the non-vacation vacation, where supposedly relaxing city dwellers stay connected to their jobs with cell phones and Wi-Fi and texting. Like others, I've been guilty of turning my Up North vacation into an Up North work-cation, which, frankly, is a waste of a good weekend at the lake.

So to put relaxation back in vacation, this schedule is what a real Up North vacation at a resort should look and feel like, starting with Friday.

6 PM: Arrive after long drive. Register at lodge, sign guest book, admire fish taxidermy. Let kids run around, throw pinecones, walk to the beach. Unload groceries. Start fire in grill or barbecue, roast hot dogs, and break out cherry Kool-Aid and potato chips. Send kids out again after dinner. Walk down to the lake to make a few casts for walleyes.

9 PM: Roast marshmallows over campfire and make s'mores. Let kids run around to burn off sugar. Break out playing cards.

10 PM to midnight: Tell a ghost story to the kids around campfire. Send them to bed. Hold hands with your spouse or partner and sit on the deck in the darkness or walk down to the lake. Look at stars and listen to loons.

2:05 AM: Wake up to loons singing. Step outside and catch a breath of fresh air. Suck in smell of pines. Go back to bed.

Saturday, 6 AM: Wake up to silence or the purr of a boat motor at the dock. Take the dog out for a brisk walk or go for a morning fishing trip.

7 AM: Eat breakfast. Good menu is sausage, scrambled eggs, toast with lots of butter. Maybe pancakes on an ancient griddle you find in the cupboard. Drink copious

amounts of black coffee. Step outside and suck in the smell of pines.

8:30 AM: Go fishing, golfing, or hiking. Take kids with you or let them head to the beach for swimming. Put tea bags in a jar and make sun tea on the deck.

Noon: Lunch. Cold sandwiches and potato salad and Jello. Fillet fish. Get extra firewood for the evening fire. Get fishing reports from other anglers or make plans to visit other golf courses. Stop by lodge and play a game of pool or pinball. Hang kids' swimsuits on deck rail. Throw tennis ball into the lake for the dog to retrieve. Of course, dog refuses to stop retrieving until you stop throwing.

1:30 PM: Nap or play cards or pull kids behind boat in inner tube. Lie on the dock with the kids and watch minnows below.

3:30 PM: Clean out boat or watch kids swim. Make sand castles at the beach. Take a kayak out for a lake tour. Ride your bike into town. Visit lodge and buy an ice cream cone. Admire lodge's taxidermy. Play a round of pool.

5 PM: Take the boat for a spin around the lake or for an evening fishing trip. Sweep sand out of the kitchen. Make a bowl of ambrosia salad. Break out pickle dish and serve homemade dills.

6 PM: Have a fish fry. Invite family from neighboring cabin for dinner. Sit in a wicker chair in screened porch and drink iced tea. Tune into a Twins baseball game on the radio.

8 PM: Enjoy the sunset. Start evening campfire. Discuss crappie-fishing or golf-putting tactics. Pull out map of local trails.

10 PM: Put kids to bed. Go for a nighttime swim. Listen to the loons. Read a well-worn Robert Ludlum spy novel before turning off the lights.

10:01 PM: Listen to the loons. Daydream about retirement.

Sunday, 6 AM: Wake to the purr of an outboard motor. Sleep in or go fishing again for a few fish to take home.

8 AM: Breakfast of bacon and eggs. Sit on porch and drink coffee. Swing by resort to see if they have a Sunday newspaper and to buy a postcard. Read a few more chapters of Robert Ludlum novel.

10 AM: Put on a cold swimsuit and head to the beach with the kids for a morning swim. Swim out to the raft and lie in the sun. Have cannonball contest with the kids.

Noon: Lunch. Finish off any leftovers; no need to pack them for home. Start packing for the trip home. Take the indefatigable dog to the beach for more retrieving. Let the dog roll in the sand and get dirty before one final retrieve. Tune into a Twins afternoon game on the radio.

Afternoon: A final fishing trip, bike ride, or round of golf. Listen to the Twins on the radio.

4 PM: Final stop at the lodge to buy a sweatshirt and trinkets for the kids.

4:15 PM: Start the first round of "99 Bottles of Beer on the Wall" for the long drive home.

Plant and Tend a Native Prairie

I've HIKED ACROSS PRAIRIES, some restored and some never touched by the plow, throughout Minnesota and the Midwest. I've hunted for pheasants, sharp-tailed grouse, and prairie chickens on these prairies and watched bison and prong-horned antelope roam across them, too. I've camped on them, taken naps on them, and gotten face to face with them, on my hands and knees, to scrutinize grasses and forbs up close. Native prairies can have more than two hundred species of plants growing in them. There is a lot to see and appreciate about prairies. They are our rarest native ecosystem, but with luck and patience, we can restore them on both a large and small scale, even in our backyards.

Why Prairie?

Less than 2 percent of Minnesota's native prairie remains, but there is a growing interest in restoring prairies. Some of these restorations involve turning cropland back into prairie; others are small plots restored by homeowners around farms or urban homes. Prairies are attractive, with their tall grasses and cornucopia of flowering forbs, but they also create a biodiversity on a landscape unlike any other. They attract beneficial insects, like bees and other pollinators, along with songbirds and mammals. A yard prairie is a low-maintenance alternative to sod and grass. It doesn't need herbicide or fertilizer. Prairies help to reduce erosion and capture nutrients that would end up in lakes and rivers. The plants' unusually deep roots effectively store carbon. Prairies are a living link to Minnesota's past.

Planning Is Critical

Restoring a prairie is nothing to rush into. It takes patience and planning. Some prairie plants take three to five years to establish themselves, requiring a long view by the planter. Mowing or burning the prairie, which naturally rejuvenates the plants, is part of the long-term maintenance strategy for a prairie.

Because some communities have rules about how high grass can be kept, check with your city, township, or county officials before planting a prairie, especially around your home. Burning your prairie might also cause concern among neighbors or local officials; check local regulations. Prairie plants need six to ten hours of sunshine, so you'll need to pick a sunny, open area for your prairie. You may want to cut trees to provide the optimal sunshine. You might also want to plan trails through your prairie, which provide handy fire breaks when you burn your prairie. Do you want a bench, birdfeeder, or wetland in your prairie? These will require planning and strategic placement. Do you want to attract wildlife and birds? You might want to select plants that provide seeds favored by wildlife.

What is the size of the prairie you want to restore, and what is your budget? These are two important considerations to make, whether you decide to restore a prairie yourself or hire a contractor. You can save money by doing the project yourself. One way to save money is to plant a portion of the prairie first and then harvest your own seed to expand the prairie. Drawing a map of your proposed prairie is a good way of organizing trails and other features, as well as groupings of certain plants. A journal will help you keep track of your maturing prairie.

Site Preparation

Prairie enthusiasts—and any experienced gardener—will tell you that site preparation by clearing away unwanted vegetation is critical to increasing your odds of a successful planting. Site preparation involves removing any unwanted sod, competing weeds, and nonnative plants that might outcompete prairie grasses and forbs. Surprisingly, many prairie manuals recommend destroying unwanted plants by applying an herbicide, such as glyphosate, commonly sold under the brand name Roundup, which doesn't leave a residue. You can also use mechanical removal, but it is time consuming and not always effective. Both methods—herbicide and mechanical removal—can be used in stages to reduce the amount of chemicals you use on the land. If your plot has brush or scrub trees, you might have to be more aggressive cutting and pulling up roots.

The final step is preparing a good seedbed. In small plots, a Rototiller works well to break the soil to one to four inches in depth. However, your goal is to have a firm seedbed so seeds are in direct contact with soil. Some restorations require a roller to pack down the soil before planting. When you walk across the prepared soil, your footprints should be no more than one to two inches deep. You don't want the seed to be buried too deeply, which inhibits proper germination.

Planting: The Right Seeds

Buy high-quality seed suited for your local area. Consult with other homeowners who have restored prairies or a local Department of Natural Resources or county biologist for recommendations. Be careful of buying seed from the shelves of national retailers that might not be suitable for your eco-region. Local native plant nurseries are knowledgeable about prairie mixes suitable for your area. A good seed mix should include both grasses and forbs, which are flowering plants. Some manuals recommend a mix with 50 to 60 percent forbs. Some common grasses are big bluestem and Indian grass. Some common forbs are black-eyed Susan, coneflowers, common ox-eye, coreopsis, and goldenrod.

According to the DNR's prairie guide, *Going Native: A Prairie Restoration Handbook for Minnesota Landowners*, the optimal time to plant prairie seed in Minnesota is late May to mid-July. If you're tending a large area, seeds can be planted using a native-seed drill pulled behind a tractor. Such drills can be rented or purchased. Some smaller versions can be pulled behind an all-terrain vehicle. Smaller plots can be seeded by hand broadcasting, but be careful not to broadcast the seed too thickly. Native plants don't require extra nitrogen, so fertilizing does more to encourage weeds.

Maintenance

Most prairies plants are perennials. In the first year, the seeds will germinate, but most growth occurs in the roots. The lack of above-ground growth can leave homeowners disappointed, but hang in there. Remember: your prairie's strong root system is what makes it resilient to drought and mostly maintenance free. During this time,

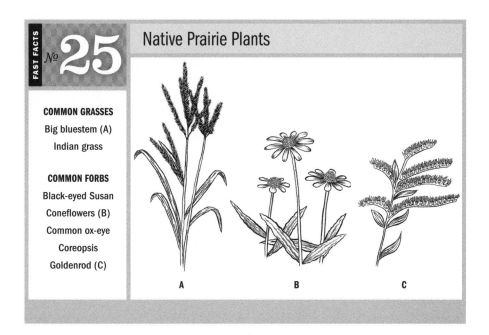

FAST FACTS

№ 25

Native Prairie Plants

COMMON GRASSES
Big bluestem (A)
Indian grass

COMMON FORBS
Black-eyed Susan
Coneflowers (B)
Common ox-eye
Coreopsis
Goldenrod (C)

A   B   C

hand weeding is a good way to get rid of unwanted plants. Mature prairies need to be burned regularly to yield better growth and more flowers. It's good to burn in sections so as to protect overwintering insects.

Familiar Words in Dakota and Ojibwe

WHILE COMMON EUROPEAN LANGUAGES are taught in high schools and some Minnesotans may even be fluent in one or more of them, very few people know anything about the languages spoken by the state's Native American tribes, the Dakota and the Ojibwe. That is too bad. These complex but highly descriptive languages are responsible for many commonly used words and place names that are integral to Minnesota geography and history. For instance, the word *Minnesota* is Dakota, meaning whitish-tinted water (*mni*, water, and *sota*, somewhat clouded), and is the name of the largest river wholly within the state's borders. The Minnesota River, as anyone who has stood by it in spring knows, becomes whitish cloudy during flood stage.

Ojibwe has given English some colorful and important words as well. They include *chickadee, toboggan, muskeg, papoose, wigwam, moose,* and *moccasin,* says Ojibwe scholar, author, and Bemidji State University professor Anton Treuer.

Unfortunately, Dakota and Ojibwe are endangered languages. The number of fluent speakers of both languages is small and grows smaller each year as elders pass away. According to a 2011 report to the Minnesota legislature, virtually no one who speaks Ojibwe or Dakota as their first language has standard teaching credentials; moreover, the languages are rarely taught formally to students in grades nine through twelve. However, there has been a new interest in student immersion programs for the languages and there are growing lists of online dictionaries and other resources.

Basics of Ojibwe

Ojibwe has roots in the Algonquian language family, which is traced to a group of Native Americans who lived in the eastern part of North America and eventually spread throughout the continent. At least twenty-seven Native American languages are part of this group, and the Ojibwe most closely share a language and cultural history with the Cree, Ottawa, and Potawatomi tribes. That said, Ojibwe has diverged significantly from those languages and is related in the same way Spanish and Portuguese have similar roots. Ojibwe has further evolved into distinct dialects. In addition to Minnesota, these dialects are spoken primarily in Wisconsin, Michigan, and parts of central Canada.

Ojibwe is highly descriptive, especially when it comes to place names and key elements of Ojibwe culture. The Ojibwe hold great respect for age, thus the name for an elder, *gichi-aya'aa,* means "great being." Geographical and animal names are rich in detail. For example, the name *Bemidji* means "where the river cuts across," says Treuer, reflecting the fact that the Bemidji region sits atop a continental divide, with the Mississippi River flowing south through Lake Bemidji and other rivers flowing west to the Red River and eventually to Hudson Bay. The word for wild rice, *manoomin,* "literally means the good crop," says Treuer.

"I think language is a great way to approach an understanding of things that were important to the Ojibwe people," he says.

While the Ojibwe language still needs support, more school immersion programs and other resources are emerging to keep it alive. The University of Minnesota has launched an online Ojibwe dictionary, including a digitally recorded pronunciation guide. In the town of Bemidji, an important hub in Ojibwe country, businesses have begun to post signage in Ojibwe. Don't be surprised if when you leave a coffee shop, a sign greets you with the word *miigwech*, which is Ojibwe for "thank you."

Basics of Dakota

The Dakota language has its foundations with the tribes of southern Minnesota, North and South Dakota, northern Nebraska, northeastern Montana, and parts of southern Canada. Like Ojibwe, Dakota is an endangered language, perhaps even more so. Fewer than thirty elders in Minnesota's four Dakota communities whose first language is Dakota remain alive. Fewer than six thousand people can speak the language at some level, according to the 2004 book *550 Dakota Verbs* by Harlan LaFontaine and Neil McKay.

Dakota has highly regionalized dialects. The dialects of eastern Montana and the western Dakotas are different from those of the eastern Dakotas, and similarly the Minnesota dialects differ from all of them. Dakota speakers from those regions understand each other, but there might be confusing expressions, much like someone speaking English from the Deep South might not be fully understood by a midwesterner. In fact, the dialects—Dakota, Lakota, and Nakota—have evolved to the point that they are considered different languages. For example, the word for "eagle" in Dakota is *wambdi*; in Lakota, it is *wambli*.

In Dakota, verbs are highly important, hence the value of an entire book devoted to them. (The authors say their goal is to reach a thousand verbs for a future book.) Unlike in English, pronouns become a direct part of the Dakota verb. For instance, the verb "to row a canoe" is *watopa*, and to say "I row a canoe" is *watowapa*. This trait is true of many European languages as well.

Descriptive Dakota words are found throughout Minnesota. *Minnetonka*, for instance, means big water, and *Chanhassen* means birch trees. Two common Dakota names signify birth order: *Chaska* comes from the Dakota word *Caske*, which means oldest son or first-born male, and *Winona* (Wiŋona) means oldest daughter or first-born female.

Efforts to protect the Dakota language are under way, including classes taught by native speakers, workbooks like *Beginning Dakota* by Nicolette Knudson, Jody Snow, and Clifford Canku, and websites with pronunciation guides and links to cultural events. In Minnesota, where so many place names are imbued with the spirit of Dakota words, younger generations are breathing new life into the language.

Put a Fish House on a Lake

I WAS TWELVE when my father and I unloaded a pile of plywood and two-by-two boards in our backyard and began building a fish house. After several days of sawing and pounding nails, we had our fishing castle for the ice, but it probably looked more like a boxy, uninspired woodshed. It was very heavy, requiring several men to lift it into our pickup truck, and after several seasons on our local lake, it was permanently located in the woods behind our house, where paper wasps and woodchucks became its only residents.

Today's fish houses are a marvel of design and comfort. While do-it-yourselfers are still building fish houses from raw materials, the modern ice-fishing shelter is more likely made of high-tech, heat-retaining fabric or insulated aluminum walls and might cost from two hundred to thirty thousand dollars. If you want to put a fish house or shelter on a lake, one is available that fits your needs and budget.

» TENT SHELTERS. These shelters take a page from modern tent design by incorporating spring-loaded aluminum or fiberglass poles. Folded, they can easily be pulled on a sled or carried on a lake and then erected in a matter of minutes. They are often designed with curved walls to shed wind and multilayered fabric walls to retain heat. They can be held to the ice with ice screws and rope tethers. Some are large enough to house six or more anglers. They can cost as little as $150.

» SLED SHELTERS. A plastic sled is incorporated into the shelter design. Once you pull the sled to your favorite ice-fishing spot, the attached fabric shelter with metal poles can be flipped open and laid snug to the ice. Most come with molded chairs or benches attached to the sled. Sled shelters can be pulled by hand or towed behind a snowmobile or all-terrain vehicle.

» Wheeled fish houses. Towed behind a vehicle, wheeled fish houses eliminate the biggest hurdle my father and I faced with our homemade fish house: getting it on and off the lake. Today's wheeled fish houses are pulled onto the lake and mechanically lowered to the ice, often with hydraulic jacks. The aluminum-walled houses come with built-in stoves, bunks, and sometimes kitchen accessories. Floor portals have removable hatches for drilling holes into the ice.

» The fish-house recreation trailers. These are super-sized, wheeled fish houses that are essentially four-season recreational trailers. Some are up to thirty feet long, outfitted with kitchens, multiple bunks, televisions, and stereo systems. The idea is a beefed-up recreational trailer that can be used in the summer but then towed onto a frozen lake for an ultra-comfortable ice-fishing experience. Expect to spend fifteen to thirty thousand dollars or more.

Knowing Clouds and Weather

Daily weather watchers can learn a lot from the television news and from noting the temperature on their car dashboard, but cloud observation has the advantage of being awe inspiring and instructive. Clouds—their heights and shapes—can tell you a lot about the weather. Where I live, I know that an east wind and nimbostratus clouds mean spending a rainy day indoors (and not mowing the lawn), whereas cumulonimbus clouds rolling in from the west on a summer evening mean a thunderstorm is inevitable, and I might get the lawn mowed before getting wet.

Cloud names are created by combining a descriptive name of a cloud shape with a name that describes its height. For example, *cirros* or *cirro* describes high clouds, while *cumulus* describes the shape—puffy. *Nimbus* or *nimbo*, when combined with *cumulus* or *stratus*, indicates clouds that are puffy and rain producing or flat or sheet rain clouds.

Clouds

CIRRUS CLOUDS

Cirrus clouds are high altitude clouds, twenty thousand feet or higher, made of ice crystals and appearing in white filaments, narrow bands, or white patches. But the so-called thunderstorm "anvil" at the top of a thunderstorm cloud is a type of cirrus cloud. Cirrus is the most common of high clouds and generally means fair weather.

CIRROCUMULUS appear as round, white puffs; they may have small ripples and may be referred to as a "mackerel" sky. Cirrocumulus are mostly seen in the winter months and indicate cold but fair weather.

CIRROSTRATUS appear as a thin, fibrous veil, often covering the entire sky and producing a halo effect around the sun or moon. They can indicate rain or snow arriving within the next twelve to twenty-four hours.

ALTO CLOUDS

Alto clouds occupy a medium zone in the sky, from eight thousand to twenty thousand feet, and they tend to predict weather changes during the following six to twelve hours.

ALTOCUMULUS clouds are grayish-white and are larger and darker than cirrocumulus or stratocumulus clouds. On a warm and humid morning, altocumulus clouds may predict a thunderstorm later in the day.

ALTOSTRATUS clouds are medium-height clouds made of water droplets that cover the entire sky. They appear ahead of storms that will bring continuous rain or snow.

Other Weather Described

» A WALL CLOUD. Typically associated with the south or southwest side of thunderstorms, wall clouds may exhibit powerful upward motions and rotation and should be watched for sustained rotation and violent winds.

» STRAIGHT-LINE WINDS. Straight-line winds are strong and even damaging winds associated with thunderstorms that don't exhibit rotation.

» DOWNDRAFTS. A downdraft is air that rapidly sinks toward the ground and can produce a downburst.

CUMULUS CLOUDS

Clouds that are vertically growing are cumulus. They can be small, lumpy clouds that indicate fair weather, or they can grow large, ominous, and dramatic.

CUMULOUS CONGESTUS is a large, towering cloud, but it is not quite a cumulonimbus cloud.

CUMULONIMBUS clouds are famous for their towering height, anvil shape at the top, and high amount of energy inside. They are associated with lightning, thunder, and, in some cases, violent winds or tornadoes.

STRATUS CLOUDS

Low clouds are stratus clouds that are sixty-five hundred feet or lower and form solid layers. They look wet. A stratus cloud that touches the ground is fog.

NIMBOSTRATUS clouds are dark gray with ragged undersides. Rain and snow is evident with nimbostratus clouds.

STRATOCUMULUS clouds are gray, low, and puffy and have blue sky mixed in. Rain doesn't often occur with stratocumulus clouds, but they can turn into moisture-producing nimbostratus clouds.

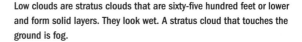

» WINDCHILL. Windchill is the "feels like" factor when temperature and wind speed impact the amount of heat loss from exposed skin. Historic low windchills aren't easy to compare because the formula to calculate windchill was changed in 2001. According to the Minnesota Climatology Working Group, one of the coldest windchills in the Twin Cities was -67°F on January 22, 1936. The old formula would have calculated it as -87°F. The temperature was -34°F with a wind speed of 20 miles per hour. Perhaps the coldest Minnesota windchill on record occurred in northern Minnesota on January 9 and 10, 1982, when temperatures plummeted to -30°F and winds were clocked at 40 miles per hour. The windchill was -71°F with the new formula and -100° F with the old.

» DEW POINT. Dew point measures moisture in the atmosphere. A high dew point indicates lots of moisture in the air, which feels "hotter" and more uncomfortable. The Minnesota summer of 2011 set a mugginess record on July 19 with an 88 degree dew point temperature measured at Moorhead, breaking the old record of 86 set on July 23, 2005. That summer, 2011, was particularly uncomfortable in the Twin Cities, which had 103 consecutive hours of dew point temperatures of 75 or higher, the longest time ever.

» SUPER CELL. A super cell is a rare but highly organized thunderstorm with excessive violence, super-sized hail, and strong to violent tornadoes.

» DERECHO. A derecho (day-ray-cho) is a very large thunderstorm and wind event associated with damaging, straight-line winds. Minnesota's most famous derecho was the July 4, 1999, storm that hit the Boundary Waters Canoe Area Wilderness with 80 to 100 mile an hour winds and leveled tens of millions of trees. In devastating the forest, the storm created new wildlife habitat but left woody debris piles vulnerable to huge wildfires for years to come.

Canning Green Beans like Your Grandmother

FOOD CANNING is in my Scandinavian and German heritage. I remember both my grandmothers canning jam and green beans, and my mother carried on the tradition when we moved west. She canned peaches, cherries, and blackberry jam, among other things. A few summers ago, when I planted three rows of bush green beans, my wife warned me that they might take over the garden.

"No worries," I said brightly. "I'll just can the ones we don't eat."

Then that ominous day arrived in late July. We'd had fresh green beans for dinner five out of the past six days. I went out to the garden, and hundreds of long, graceful pods clung to my bush beans like slender green pencils. They were becoming vermin.

"Time to break out the pressure cooker," I whispered, "and put these babies up for the winter."

Canning Low-Acid Food

Green beans, along with most vegetables other than tomatoes, must be canned in a pressure canner because they are low-acid foods. They have a pH level greater than 4.6, which means they have little acid to guard against spoilage-creating bacteria.

To reach a temperature to kill potentially dangerous bacteria, you must steam-pressure low-acid foods at 240°F (at or below a thousand feet above sea level). The steam-pressure canner is able to achieve that higher temperature, unlike a water-bath canner. If you're higher than a thousand feet, you increase the pressure in the canner to achieve the high temperature.

Many people are wary of pressure canners because they've heard vague stories that the appliance can explode in a ball of high-pressure steam. I had received a pressure canner for Christmas, quickly read the instructions, and began using it to can and cook foods. These modern cookers are actually quite safe if you follow the directions and pay attention to your pressure gauge.

After gathering more canning information from my mother and grandmother, I procured some hand-me-down jars from my mother-in-law and some basic equipment from a hardware store: a jar lifter, a magnetic lid lifter, lids, and bands.

After fresh green beans threatened to take over our garden and kitchen, my wife was impressed when I produced fourteen jars of canned green beans in a Saturday afternoon. "They look so pretty," she said, admiring the jars on the counter. "Just like the ones my grandmother made."

Here's How It's Done

» JAR PREP. I used wide-mouth quart jars, ran them through the dishwasher, and checked them for nicks and cracks around the rim. I purchased new lids and bands for the jars and made sure they were free of dents. Before prepping the green beans, I put my jars into a vat of hot water and simmered them at about 180 degrees. I also put the lids in a saucepan of hot, but not boiling, water.

» GREEN BEAN PREP. I selected only the freshest and most tender green beans. I selected ones that were the straightest and uniform in size so they would go more easily into the jar. I washed them well and trimmed the ends.

I chose the raw-pack method, which means you can the beans without blanching them first. Some canning books recommend dipping the beans in hot water for five minutes; others advocate packing them uncooked and raw into jars.

» PACKING THE JARS. I packed the beans into the jars, shaking each jar during the process to orient the beans vertically for optimal space usage. Pour boiling water into the jar until the beans are covered, leaving one inch of head space, which is the space between the top of the water level and the jar lid. Slide a plastic spatula around the inside of the jar, between the beans and the jar wall, and gently remove any air bubbles. Once any bubbles are removed, wipe the rim with clean cotton cloth for optimal seal, and place a lid (from your saucepan of hot water) on the jar. Screw the band on the jar and tighten with your fingertips until the lid doesn't turn.

Most pressure canners can handle seven jars at a time. While I'm preparing the jars, I've kept the canner prepped with hot water on the stove. The canner is filled with only about two inches of water. Place the packed jars into the canner.

Lock the canner lid in place, and follow the canner instructions for bringing it to a boil and adjusting the vent. Bring the canner to 10 pounds of pressure for altitudes at or below 1,000 feet (check your canner instructions for adjusting above 1,000 feet). Keep the pressure steady at 10 pounds, and cook the beans for 20 minutes for pints

FAST FACTS

№ 27

Canned Green Beans

Canned food, like green beans, that is properly preserved will keep its optimum eating quality for at least one year, provided the food is stored in a cool, dry place.

National Center for Home Food Preservation

and 25 minutes for quarts. Start counting only after the pressure gauge reaches 10 pounds. (This for a weighted-gauge pressure canner. For a dial-gauge canner, begin counting after the gauge reaches 11 pounds.)

Allow the canner to return to 0 pounds of pressure. Don't toy with the vent; it's crucial to allow the canner to return to 0 naturally. Wait a few minutes and then remove the lid. Let the jars cool further and then place them on the countertop on a dry towel. Give them room so cool air can circulate around them. Don't try to tighten the bands. Let the jar cool for 12 hours or overnight.

Once jars are cool, tap the lids and check for a proper seal. The lid should be pulled down, or concave, and won't flex. Store jars in a cool, dry area.

Carving a Duck Decoy

I N THE BEGINNING, wooden duck decoys were never meant for the auction houses like Sotheby's or Christie's. Duck hunters wanted a utilitarian wooden duck that would fool mallards, pintails, and bluebills. Decoy makers knew this—most were duck hunters themselves—and they went to work in their basements, garages, and, later, small factories to hew wooden birds with their own unique qualities.

When it came to selling their decoys, the makers said, "This bird will work better than Joe's," and the duck hunters ran their fingers over the wood, examined the shape and form, and said, "Yep, this will work." When they brought home a brace of dead waterfowl, which meant food for the table, they spread the word, and the reputation of a decoy maker grew.

This was true in Minnesota, where market hunting supplied ducks for the masses in big midwestern cities in the late nineteenth and early twentieth centuries, and where later a bounty of ducks drew legions of sport hunters when market hunting became illegal.

Along the way, the tides shifted. Plastic and foam decoys, mass produced cheaply in factories, became de rigueur; the old masters died, and their decoys became

Marty Hanson decoys

recognized as works of art, sometimes selling for tens of thousands of dollars. Ironically, as the wooden decoy became artistic treasure—and with the invention of plastic decoys—fewer people continued carving them by hand.

Marty Hanson of Prior Lake is one of those still carving. As a kid, he admired the Mason decoys in his grandfather's basement for their form and function. At age eleven, Hanson decided to try his hand at carving his own wooden ducks. Like the old masters, his reputation grew as he made more wooden birds. When he was fifteen, he was making up to thirty birds a week while he held a job at the Minneapolis Gun Club. When he was twenty, he left the house one morning without any money but with a car full of hand-carved decoys. He returned later that day with $900 in cash. "To a guy who was twenty and loved decoys, $900 in cash in your pocket was a lot of money," he says. "That's when I decided to go full time."

Hanson doesn't know exactly how many wooden decoys he has made, but the number is likely approaching eight thousand. During one period in his life, he made about three hundred decoys a year, which is extraordinary considering he carves them by hand and uses a minimal number of power tools. His production has waned over the years as demand for his decoys has spilled into the collector and vintage market. His prices have risen, and he has also developed a business appraising and selling antique decoys. But he represents one of the last links to a storied past: a decoy carver who makes "gunning" decoys that are cherished not just for their artistry but for their ability to fool ducks.

» THE WOOD: He began making decoys from western red cedar that he bought at the lumberyard but became pickier as his understanding of wood and desire for better decoys grew. Now he handpicks his wood from select cuts of white cedar, a species native to Minnesota.

» THE TOOLS: Hanson uses spoke shaves, draw knives, files, and other hand knives. The only power tools he uses are a drill press and band saw. He paints his decoys by hand.

» WHY HE AVOIDS MOST POWER TOOLS: Hanson dislikes power tools because they are loud and create a lot of dust, which would take extra time to manage in his shop and isn't good for a carver's lungs. Besides, Hanson is fast with a knife—perhaps faster than using a power tool—creating the traditional, rough-hewn look that is his trademark and harkens to past masters. "My style is a traditional surface. I finish it all by hand, either with a scraper or with a knife, sometimes a file. Sandpaper is a carver's nightmare. With sandpaper, it's gradual. I can get the same result with two or three swipes with my knife."

» HOW HE LEARNED: Hanson is self-taught. He was always sketching pictures as a child but never attended art school. He went to college for a year and a half to study biology but found his calling was carving. He learned by studying other decoys and ducks in the wild but mostly by doing through trial and error.

» ART AND HUNTING MERGE: "Hunting was a big part of the draw for me," Hanson says. He was a duck hunter first, drawn to the marshes in pursuit of mallards and other ducks with his family members. But he also had a talent for art and an appreciation for history.

"As a kid, I always drew and this was something that I could make out of wood," he says. "I didn't think about the tradition; I just thought it was cool that my grandfather's and father's decoys were made in the 1920s and 30s, and they were really old."

» THE DECOY FORM AND STYLE: Hunters are looking for a decoy that, when viewed from the farthest possible distance, accurately portrays a species of duck. Hanson says the best decoy is something that exaggerates the bird's form and makes a good silhouette from a distance. "You can put a hundred hours of work into the detail on it, but if you back up thirty yards away, all that detail is lost. That's the most important thing with form; it has to be something appealing to the eye and simple in form."

When Hanson began carving, his clients were not concerned about refinements in the decoy; they were concerned about how well the wooden decoy rode in the water, whether the anchor strings would stay on them in storage, and their durability in the hunting scenario. However, after carving thousands of decoys, Hanson's style changed, he says, "from the crude utilitarian style to the artistic style. I'm doing more standing birds and still lifes. They are decorative forms of art, but it is still a traditional style of decoy that uses traditional carving methods." Hanson says the masters changed their style over their careers, too.

» STILL ROOM FOR NEW CARVERS: Hanson believes there are opportunities for young carvers to make a name for themselves. "You can make $200 birds, there is a market for that, but it has to be quality. For me it's been a thirty-five-year journey. People can't carve for five or six years and expect to reach that level." He says it helps to be knowledgeable in business and the rules of supply and demand. You don't want to make too many decoys and not have enough demand. "Every decoy you make is a business card," he says. "The longer you stick with it, the more successful you'll be. But quality is of first and foremost importance."

The Tunnel of Fudge Cake

O UR HOMAGE to a fudgy icon started with a question.

"Three and a half sticks of butter?" I asked. "Holy cow."

My sixteen-year-old stepdaughter, Bailey, and I were examining a recipe for the holy grail of Minnesota baking recipes—the Tunnel of Fudge Cake. In 1966 Ella

Helfrich filled a Bundt pan with her thick concoction of butter, sugar, cocoa powder, and, yes, three and a half sticks of butter and made history.

Her Tunnel of Fudge Cake took second place in the Pillsbury Bake-Off Contest and sent homemakers scrambling to buy a Bundt pan, which had been invented sixteen years earlier by Minnesotan H. David Dalquist. (Pillsbury was also a Minnesota company at the time.) Dalquist and his wife, Dorothy, had started the Nordic Ware company in 1946 in Minneapolis, and until then, the company had flown largely under the culinary radar, making cookware for Scandinavian cookies and other ethnic cooking.

In 1950, David Dalquist designed the Bundt pan at the request of members of the Minneapolis Chapter of the Hadassah Society. They had ceramic cake pans with designs but wanted something made of modern aluminum.

Dalquist's Bundt pan wasn't a huge seller, but then a frosted bolt of lightning struck. By taking second in the national baking contest (and winning five thousand dollars), Helfrich, a Texan, brought instant fame to her cake and the Bundt pan and set Nordic Ware on a course to sell sixty million of the sturdy, ridged pans over the next forty-five years.

Baking is not my forte, which is why I enlisted Bailey to help me re-create Helfrich's cake. As a youngster, she learned baking at her mother's elbow, but as a teen, she struck off on her own culinary journey, trying new recipes and entire dinners of sloppy joes and chili. She was naturally curious about my story of the Tunnel of Fudge Cake.

Whenever the baking accoutrements are spread across the counter in our kitchen, a crowd gathers. Daughter Grace, age eight, saw the cocoa and sugar, and she began lingering nearby, wondering aloud if she would get to lick the mixer beaters. It was a late January evening and spitting sleet outside, and the likelihood of a warm oven and fudgy cake seemed to buoy everyone's spirits.

It is not hard to find a Tunnel of Fudge recipe; there are several on the Internet, and the book *Bundt Cake Bliss*, a celebration of calories in the shape of a Bundt ring, contains the old standard. All the recipes I found highlighted the Tunnel of Fudge's appeal: the somewhat mysterious appearance of a soft, gooey center in the cake. It didn't seem much of a mystery to me because all the recipes caution not to bake beyond 45 or 50 minutes, suggesting the center is simply left slightly undercooked.

№28   The Tunnel of Fudge Cake

Heat oven to 350 degrees. Prepare a 12-cup Bundt pan by coating the inside with butter and sprinkling with cocoa powder.

Cake: Combine flour and cocoa powder and set aside. Using an electric mixer, combine sugar and butter until light and fluffy. Add eggs one at a time and mix thoroughly. Add the 2 cups of confectioners' sugar and blend thoroughly. Add the flour and cocoa mixture and mix by hand until well blended. Stir in walnuts [Note: several modern cookbooks and Internet recipes offer nutless versions of the cake.]

Pour the thick batter into the prepared pan, making sure it is evenly distributed. Bake for 45 minutes or until the top is set and edges are beginning to pull from sides of pan. There is no need to use a toothpick to determine doneness. You want the inside to be soft, and if there is a mistake to be made with the cake, it is overcooking.

Cool upright in pan on wire rack for 1½ hours to allow fudge to set. Turn upside down onto serving plate and cool completely, at least 2 hours.

Glaze: mix confectioners' sugar and cocoa with 4 tablespoons of milk or half-and-half. Mix thoroughly and gradually add only enough milk so the glaze is pourable. Spoon the glaze over the cake, making sure it runs down the sides and between the ridges. Cake can be stored at room temperature for several days.

CAKE

2¼	cups flour
¾	cup cocoa powder (preferably Dutch cocoa)
1¾	cups white granulated sugar
1¾	cups softened butter
6	eggs
2	cups confectioners' sugar
2	cups chopped walnuts

GLAZE

¾	cup confectioners' sugar
¼	cup cocoa powder
4–6	teaspoons whole milk or half-and-half

With the butter softened to room temperature, Bailey began mixing in sugar—the first step—while Grace hovered nearby. Soon Bailey had a light and fluffy sugar mixture. Once the beaters were removed from the bowl, Grace scooted to the counter and received a buttery, glistening wand. Her face broke into a grin.

Much later that night, after it was past everyone's bedtime and the cake had met its mandatory one-and-a-half-hour cooling period, I turned the Bundt pan upside down and the cake slipped onto a platter. I mixed the glaze and drizzled it over the top, thinking back to Ella Helfrich and how this concoction of confectioners' sugar and cocoa must have changed her life. Helfrich didn't win the contest in 1966 (first place went to Mari Petrelli of Ely, Nevada, with a Golden Gate Snack Bread), but the Texas baker must have felt in some way that she had won the lottery.

Nearly fifty years have passed, but the inspirations of two strangers, inventor H. David Dalquist and baker Ella Helfrich, had melded once again in my kitchen. I slipped a knife into the ring of chocolate cake and drew out a sizable piece. A tunnel of fudge, still slightly warm, glistened at the center of the slice, and I attacked it with my fork.

I didn't really care to speculate how it got there.

A Short Guide to Urban Bicycling

ADD URBAN BICYCLING and bicycle commuting to the growing list of skills practiced by Minnesotans.

According to Minneapolis officials, the city ranks second nationally in the number of bicyclists, as measured by the U.S. Census Bureau. *Bicycling Magazine* picked Minneapolis as the best biking city in the country. St. Paul has not earned such plaudits, but the city's comprehensive plan calls for Minnesota's capital to "become a world-class bicycling city" that "encourages bicycle use as a part of everyday life."

This two-wheel ambition reaches statewide, too. In 2010 Minnesota was ranked the fourth most "bicycle friendly" state by the League of American Bicyclists.

№ 29   Interest in Bicycling Is Growing

MINNEAPOLIS

Increase in the number of Bicyclists, 2007–11

47%

Bicycling commuting has significantly gained in popularity, though numbers are still small.

Residents who commute by bicycle

4%

Of those,

37%

are women.

City's planners have set a goal of

178 miles

of bikeways by 2015.

As of 2011, there were only eleven miles left to add.

Woman with "electric" bicycle, 1890s

Urban planners, particularly in Minneapolis and St. Paul, have heeded the call for bike-friendly environs. They are devoting more resources to creating bike trails and dedicated bike lanes on city streets and to other bicycling resources such as bike lockers for commuters, maps, and a seat at the planning table. In 2011 Minneapolis hired a bicycle and pedestrian program coordinator.

Equipment

When choosing an urban commuting bicycle, consider the distance of your ride, the type of terrain you'll encounter, and whether you'll ride unpaved roads and commute in the winter. Road bikes, those lightweight and sleek bikes, are great for paved roads; their narrow tires reduce resistance, giving you a faster ride. Their narrow tires, however, aren't good on unpaved surfaces and give little traction (unless fitted with specialty tires) on icy roads. Moreover, you may not want to use an expensive road bike in winter conditions because of the corrosive nature of water, sand, and salt.

Mountain bikes have wider tires and provide a more stable ride—they're ideal for winter riding—and are good for paved and unpaved conditions. However, they tend to be heavier than road bikes and won't be as energy efficient either. Some commuters find a better fit with hybrid or cross bikes that have characteristics of both road and mountain bikes: an upright ride (like a mountain bike) but with a lightweight frame and narrower tires than a mountain bike.

Fenders are a great addition to commuter bikes; they fend off water that can splash on your clothes. A rear rack and panniers are ideal for carrying your work materials and spare clothes. Some commuters wear backpacks, but they can increase your sweating. Lights and reflectors are not only a good idea but required under state law.

Planning a Route

It's never been easier to plan your bicycle commuter route. Minneapolis and St. Paul have produced bicycling maps. The Metropolitan Council has suggested routes and ways you can link your bicycle route with buses, many of which have bicycle racks. The Met Council also has bike lockers for rent. All the information can be found on the city and council websites.

Use the Road

Minnesota law states bicyclists have the right to operate on streets, roads, and highways unless otherwise restricted. It is illegal to ride against traffic. Why ride on the road instead of sidewalks? Studies have shown that roads are actually safer for bicyclists than sidewalks. Bicyclists must obey rules of the road, including stopping at all stop signs and traffic lights and using hand signals to indicate turns.

FAST FACTS

№ **30**

The goal is to arrive safely at your destination. Here are some suggestions for fun and worry-free biking.

Other Urban Riding Tips

Look both ways at intersections or driveways.

Ride defensively. Keep a watch for people who may not see you. Riding aggressively only endangers your life. Bicyclists and motorists must yield the right of way to each other.

Lights, reflectors, and brightly colored and reflective clothing are essential for safe night riding. For night riding, state law requires bicyclists to use a headlight and rear reflectors. To increase visibility, add a rear flashing light.

Wear light-colored clothing that is reflective. Bright yellow is a good choice.

A well-tuned bicycle will keep you from having breakdowns on the road.

Always wear a properly fitting helmet that is fastened. According to the Share the Road program, which encourages safe bicycle riding, 91 percent of bicyclists who were killed in 2008 reportedly weren't wearing helmets.

Motorists are required to maintain a three-foot clearance while passing a bicyclist.

Winter Riding

Dress like you would for cross-country skiing or another high-aerobic winter sport. Layering starts with a wicking shirt next to your skin, followed by an insulating layer and a windproof pants and jacket on top.

Wear a thin stocking cap under your helmet and wear mittens. Some riders prefer the "lobster claw" glove that keeps fingers together for warmth but allows mobility for braking and other bike functions.

Know Your Minnesota Trails

North Shore

» THE SUPERIOR HIKING TRAIL. The hiking trail runs 227 miles along the Sawtooth Mountains and other ridges of Lake Superior, starting in Duluth and ending at the Canada border. Trailheads are located nearly every five to ten miles. Eighty-two backcountry campsites have no fees or reservation system. Quaint bridges cross streams and large rivers. The system is managed by volunteers through the Superior Hiking Trail Association.

» THE C. J. RAMSTAD/NORTH SHORE STATE TRAIL. The natural surface trail, named after a well-known Minnesota snowmobile journalist, runs 146 miles from Duluth to Grand Marais. Most of the trail offers backcountry uses mainly for snowmobilers.

Iron Range

» THE MESABI TRAIL. A paved trail that is scheduled to be 132 miles when completed, the Mesabi Trail runs between Ely and Grand Rapids. As of 2011, about 115 miles were paved. The longest paved section is 75 miles, connecting Grand Rapids and McKinley. During spring through fall, it is popular for biking, inline skating, and walking. In the winter, the trail offers cross-country skiing, snowshoeing, and winter hiking.

» THE TACONITE STATE TRAIL. Mainly a natural surface trail, the Taconite Trail is used primarily for snowmobiling in the winter. It connects Grand Rapids to Ely, intersecting the Arrowhead State Trail

» THE ARROWHEAD STATE TRAIL. The 135-mile trail is also a natural surface trail used mostly for snowmobiling. From its start at the Taconite State Trail near Tower, the Arrowhead Trail runs north to International Falls.

North-Central Minnesota

» THE PAUL BUNYAN STATE TRAIL. The trail is 112 miles long from Brainerd to Bemidji, making it the longest continuously paved trail in the state system. In the summer, the trail is popular for hiking, bicycling, and inline skating; in the winter, the trail is used for snowmobiling. According to the Department of Natural Resources, the trail is scheduled to be connected with the Blue Ox Trail, making it the longest paved trail converted from abandoned railroad tracks in North America. It will be 210 miles long.

Eastern Trails

» THE WILLARD MUNGER STATE TRAIL. The Willard Munger State Trail is several trails linking small towns along the Interstate 35 corridor between Hinckley and Duluth. The Hinckley to Duluth segment is 63 miles long and is paved. The Alex Laveau Memorial Trail connects Gary–New Duluth to Wrenshall and Carlton. The Matthew Lourey State Trail is 80 miles of natural surface trail linking St. Croix State Park with the Chengwatana, St. Croix, and Nemadji State Forests. The Matthew Lourey State Trail is used mainly for snowmobiling, horseback riding, hiking, and mountain biking.

Twin Cities Metro Trails

» LUCE LINE STATE TRAIL. Located in the west metro, the Luce Line State Trail is a limestone surface trail that runs from Plymouth to Winsted. A horse trail runs parallel to it. The 63-mile-long trail is popular for biking, running, horseback riding, snowmobiling, and cross-country skiing. Snowmobiles are allowed on the trail west of Stubb's Bay Road.

» THE GATEWAY TRAIL. The Gateway Trail begins in St. Paul and runs 18 miles through Maplewood, North St. Paul, and Oakdale. It ends at Pine Point Regional Park. A newly purchased spur will connect it with downtown Stillwater.

Southern Trails

» CASEY JONES STATE TRAIL. Three segments run through far southern Minnesota. One segment connects Pipestone and the Pipestone-Murray county line; a short second segment runs one and a half miles west of Lake Wilson; and a third is a six-mile loop between Lake Shetek State Park and Currie.

» ROOT RIVER STATE TRAIL. Starting in Fountain, the southeast Minnesota Root River State Trail runs 42 miles through bluff lands to Houston. The trail is popular for bicycling, hiking, inline skating, horseback riding, cross-country skiing, and snowmobiling.

» THE SAKATAH SINGING HILLS STATE TRAIL. The trail joins Faribault and Mankato with a paved route; a parallel trail for horseback riding runs from Lime Valley Road to Eagle Lake. Sakatah Lake State Park is along the trail.

Ski Lift Know-How

THE ACT OF SUCCESSFULLY getting on a ski lift begins before you reach the lift itself.

Once you ski to the ski-lift line, you'll scoot and push yourself along with others anxious to get back to the top of the hill. You may be in line with a companion or someone may pair up with you as the line progresses to the lift. Eventually, the line will narrow as you reach the lift, and this is where you need to pay attention.

As the skiers in front of you move forward to the lift platform, the lift operator will catch the lift or otherwise prepare it for those skiers. Once they take their position on the platform, the lift swings around the bull wheel, and the lift operator holds it steady while the skiers sit down. The operator secures them with any safety apparatus and then sends the skiers on their way.

Meanwhile you have moved forward to prepare to enter the staging area. Once the skiers in front of you have left the staging area, it is your job to move forward. Look down and you should see a permanent line or mark on the platform where you must stand to wait for the lift. Move to the line. Once the lift swings around the bull wheel, the lift operator will grab it, you sit down, and the operator will secure any safety devices.

Problems typically occur when skiers aren't paying attention. They may enter the staging area too late to catch the next lift or they might not sit properly on the lift or squirm around as it's preparing to leave the staging area. Either way, if you don't pay attention, you are apt to embarrass yourself and possibly incur the dissatisfaction of the lift operator. Operators like efficiency and flowing lines at their lifts; your job is to not screw that up.

While you're headed up the mountain, it's verboten to throw things off the lift or otherwise act in stupid or unsafe ways. After all, you could be suspended forty feet off the ground, and stunts you pull could threaten you or others with severe injury or death. Don't be a dork.

As you get close to disembarking from the lift, it's time once again to pay attention to the operator and your equipment. Make sure your gear is attached to you and not tangled in the lift. Anticipate when the lift will reach the spot where your legs are able to touch terra firma. Disembarking too early or too late can also yield embarrassment for you or displeasure from the lift operator. When your skis touch the snow, stand up briskly and ski away from the lift. If you drop something, wait until you've moved safely away from the lift to retrieve it. If the item is under the lift chair, the operator can stop the lift and snag it for you.

How to Land a Muskie

ESOX MASQUINONGY is the master of Minnesota waters, the king of fishes. The muskellunge is a freshwater barracuda, with a mouth full of teeth and a top-of-the-food-chain attitude. Anglers have reported being unnerved when, unhooking and measuring a large muskie, the fish's eyes seem to track the angler's every move. Since female muskies grow larger than males, anglers refer reverently to their biggest catches as "she," as in, "She hit my lure so hard I just about jumped out of my socks."

A big female muskie might be the freshwater equivalent to a mature lioness—a sleek, tactical, and unpredictable predator.

All of that makes the actual landing of a big muskie a bit confounding. I've interviewed dozens of anglers who have landed true trophy muskies weighing more than forty pounds and a few topping fifty pounds, and their stories rarely focus on the fight. These lucky and usually skilled anglers talk about their tactics, the monotony of cast after fruitless cast, and finally, the vicious strike, but rarely do

Proud angler, worthy fish: landing a muskie, 1925

their stories linger for long on the muskie battle. There are some reasons for this that make sense once you understand the sport of muskie fishing.

Most serious muskie anglers use heavy-duty tackle. Their rods and reels are designed to subdue any big fish quickly but also to sling the very large lures—some weighing a pound or more—hour after hour without the rods and reels breaking down. Muskies are called the fish of ten thousand casts, and anglers aren't willing to use anything other than heavy-duty tackle to subdue one. After all that work, you wouldn't want to lose a big, powerful fish because of a weak line and underperforming rod and reel. All that beefy equipment can make a muskie fight short and a bit anticlimactic.

There is another reason muskie anglers value stout equipment that can easily subdue a muskie—they don't want to overly exert the fish. A quick fight means not fighting the fish to complete exhaustion, which lessens its chances of survival after being released. True muskie anglers go to great lengths to ensure a muskie is released fresh and healthy, even using a mesh cradle to land them alongside the boat rather than lifting them out of the water. A quick fight means a muskie is more apt to live to fight another day. For muskie anglers, the rule of catch and release is immutable.

This is not to say muskie anglers take landing a muskie for granted. The first step in landing this great fish is properly setting the hook when there is a strike. Sometimes when striking a surface lure, which can gurgle and make small wakes on the water, a muskie will miss it altogether, only to turn around and strike again. It requires steely nerves for an angler to properly judge the strike and set the hook at the right time. Muskies won't often jump out of the water like a leaping bass, but they will thrash on or near the surface and maybe "throw the hooks," which isn't so much an intentional act conceived by the muskie—it is, after all, a fish with a rather small brain—but often the result of a poor hook set or the fish turning at an angle that causes the lure to detach from the fish's mouth.

Muskies are powerful fish, and the biggest ones are forty to fifty pounds of pure muscle. They can make powerful surges and swim under or around a boat, forcing the angler to keep steady pressure on the line and constantly adjust to the fish's move. If the fish swims around the boat, the angler has to follow. The tricky part is staying calm and maneuvering without stumbling or catching the line on the motor or some other part of the boat.

Once the fish is boat side, an angler wears leather or Kevlar gloves to protect his or her hands not just from sharp teeth but from hooks. A last-minute thrashing can send a sharp hook into an angler's hand, thus joining the powerfully flailing fish and angler together with dire consequences. A pair of long-nosed pliers is also essential for removing hooks without injuring the fish or the angler. This is typically a two-person operation—one holding the rod while the other unhooks the fish—but solo anglers have caught and released some large muskies on their own.

Since serious muskie anglers release virtually all the muskies they catch, taking a picture is crucial to documenting you caught a big one. Anglers will slip one hand just inside the gill plate and firmly grasp a smooth segment of the jaw without getting their hands fully inside the gills. Gills have sharp edges and can gash a hand readily, so finding the right spot for holding the fish is critical. With one hand gripping the gill plate, the other hand is slipped under the belly and the fish is usually held diagonally. Some anglers simply grab the fish with both hands and lift it vertically, but vertical pictures don't often show the true dimensions of the fish. In their excitement and desire to quickly release the fish, muskie anglers sometimes fail to get a good picture. Most, however, are able to keep still their trembling knees, get a firm grip on the fish, and capture its full beauty and dimensions.

After that, the fish is gently placed into the water, and the angler will hold its tail and keep it steady until the fish fully recovers. The entire process from strike to release can take fifteen minutes or less. It's a short, powerful dose of adrenaline, an encounter with the elusive fish that rules the waters.

Navigate a Lake

NAVIGATING A LAKE in a boat is satisfying for a singular reason: there are no roads. The freedom to head in any direction, taking into account obstacles and weather, without the constrictions of pavement or highway signs, is appealing and perhaps a bit daunting for those not used to operating outside the white lines. For a young person, driving a boat is a rite of passage. When my dad handed over the tiller to our Montgomery Ward Sea King outboard, I knew I'd passed through an important threshold to manhood.

Your great-grandfather navigated lakes by memory or by lining up landmarks along the shoreline. He might even have used a compass in big water. His lake map would likely have provided a detailed outline of the lake, but its topographic features would be crude by today's standards. Topographic mapmakers used to measure lake depths by drilling holes through the ice and dropping a string with a weight to the bottom. Estimated depths could have been off by several feet or more.

Today's lake maps are made using global positioning systems and pinpoint depth-locating equipment. Using a modern GPS navigation device and depth locator, you can track your progress and underwater features to within a few feet. Anglers can find very small areas—a subtle drop-off or small pile of rocks—within tens of thousands of acres of water using these sophisticated devices.

But what if you don't own such a device?

There is a lot of value to knowing basic lake navigation. There are several things to consider. You want to be able to reach your destination—a distant shore, island, or reef—without running aground or hitting anyone or anything else. Knowing what direction to go is important, but it is equally important to know where the underwater obstacles lie. Sometimes these obstacles are marked by a buoy, usually placed by a local enforcement agency, but others, such as stumps, are unmarked and may not appear on a map.

If You Don't Have a Map

Let's say you're headed across an unfamiliar lake, and you don't have a map (but you should). You should have a basic sense of what direction your destination lies. East, west, north, or south? Remember the sun rises in the east and sets in the west—that will give you the basics of where on the compass you are headed. If you can judge that the rising sun is on your left, you are likely facing south. If the rising sun is on your right, you are facing north.

Caution is the rule of the day if you're navigating an unfamiliar lake without navigation aids. Once you know the basic direction you need to go, it is still worthwhile to stay within eyeshot of land so you can use landmarks to help aid your navigation. Navigating without a map gets trickier if the water body has multiple bays or is oddly shaped. Go slow and keep your senses about you and continue to monitor your direction. Watch for underwater obstacles just below the waterline. Waves act differently when they wash over a shallow, submerged obstacle. Look for differences in the wave action and choppy water that might indicate a reef or submerged log.

If You Have a Map

Of course, navigating a lake with a map is much easier than without, but it doesn't guarantee you'll get to your destination without trouble. Boaters often misread maps and speed across a lake without caution to obstacles, boating lanes, and markers or other boaters.

A Few Words about Life Jackets

According to law, all boats regardless of length, including canoes, kayaks, stand-up paddleboards, and duck boats, must have a readily accessible U.S. Coast Guard–approved Type I, II, III, or V wearable personal floatation device or life jacket for each person onboard. Also, boats sixteen feet or longer (except canoes and kayaks) must have at least one Coast Guard–approved Type IV throwable device. That is the law, but it is also simply common sense to have life jackets and to wear them.

No **31** Buoy Identification

Knowing buoys and what they signal can keep you out of trouble on a lake or river. These markers can be placed by the U.S. Coast Guard, local or state law enforcement, or government agencies. While buoys are commonly used in open water, signs can also be used.

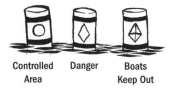

Controlled   Danger   Boats
Area   Keep Out

A white buoy or sign with an orange diamond is a danger warning to boaters. It may identify rocks or rapids or other underwater debris. The type of obstacle can be lettered in black.

BOATING CHANNEL LIES BETWEEN THESE BUOYS

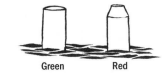

Green   Red

Solid green and solid red companion buoys indicate a boating channel lies between them. In flowing water, the red buoy is on the right side of the channel if a boater is facing upstream.

A red-and-white striped buoy indicates the center of a channel and should be passed closely on either side. A black-and-white striped buoy indicates a shoreward obstruction, and you should not pass between it and the nearest shore.

A white buoy or sign with an orange diamond and cross indicates a keep-out area for boats. The reason for the restriction is indicated in black lettering, such as "Swimming Area."

A white buoy or sign with an orange circle and black lettering indicates controlled or restricted areas, such a slow or no-wake zone. Slow or no-wake means you must operate your boat at the slowest possible speed and still maintain steerage.

Mooring buoys are all-white with a blue stripe between the top and the waterline.

Mooring

Rules of the Water

When you are on the water, rules apply to watercraft just as rules of the road apply to motorists. Here are some important rules of the water:

» PASSING. If one watercraft is overtaking another going in the same direction, the boat being overtaken must maintain its course and speed. Meanwhile, the passing watercraft must keep a sufficient distance to avoid collision or endangering the other boat with its wake.

» WATERCRAFT MEETING. When two watercraft approach each other head on, each must alter course to the right to avoid collision. If the two watercraft are far enough to the left of each other, no change in direction is needed for safe passage. Both watercraft will maintain their course and speed so as to pass clear of each other and keep to the right in narrow channels.

» WATERCRAFT CROSSING. If two watercraft are approaching at a right angle, the boat on the right has the right of way.

» BOATS WITHOUT MOTORS. Canoes, sailboats, and other non-motorized watercraft have the right of way over motorized watercraft in all situations except when a non-motorized craft is overtaking or passing.

Build a Bluebird House

THE EASTERN BLUEBIRD is a lapis-colored treasure, a brilliant blue bird of grasslands and mixed hardwood forests. You can spot them flitting near pastures and sitting on power lines; their song is an unmistakable warble. They have many fans in the bird-watching world, perhaps none bigger than the late Dick Peterson, who helped start the Bluebird Recovery Program of Minnesota in the late 1980s.

In the 1970s, Dick began tinkering with the design of bluebird houses, hoping to devise a house that was easy to build, hang, and maintain. According to the book *Woodworking for Wildlife*, by the famed nongame wildlife expert Carrol Henderson, Peterson's influence was so great that a birdhouse was named after him. The Peterson Bluebird House is considered the standard for all bluebird house designs.

The Peterson Bluebird House

The Peterson Bluebird House is constructed with only seven pieces of wood, of either cedar or pine. Three of those pieces are cut from a single two-by-four board that is thirty-six inches long. The pieces become the back, the floor, and inner roof (an outer roof covers the entire birdhouse). The other pieces are cut from one-by-four-inch and one-by-ten-inch boards. The sides are made of 7/16-inch-thick hardboard lap siding. Once the pieces are cut, the birdhouse is easily assembled with a hammer and nails:

1 Attach the inner roof two-by-four piece to the top of the back board.

2 Nail the floor piece to the back about ten and a half inches below the top edge.

3 Nail the two sides to the frame.

4 Nail the swinging door (also the front piece) with one nail through each side of the siding on the bottom. They serve as the hinges for the door. A third nail is put near the entrance hole on the top. The nail serves as a latch; it is pulled out to open the door.

5 Nail the outer roof piece

Hang the house near fields, pastures, marshes, or ditches where bluebirds have been seen. Bluebird houses should be cleaned each fall and monitored regularly. *Woodworking for Wildlife* provides detailed instructions for building and maintaining your Peterson Bluebird House.

Snowplow Truck Driving: A Career Reflection

JOHN HAGLUND experienced twenty-two winters from behind the wheel of a snowplow truck on some of Minnesota's loneliest highways. Working for the Minnesota Department of Transportation out of Baudette, along the Minnesota-Canada border, Haglund was part of a crew of five drivers who kept the roads clear of snow and ice around Baudette, west to Warroad and east to Pelland. Haglund's main route, however, was a fifty-five-mile stretch of Minnesota 72 that runs like an arrow south from Baudette to Waskish and Kelliher. The highway traverses some of the most remote countryside outside federal wilderness areas, surrounded by swamps, aspen forests, and a few farm fields. In the many times I've driven this stretch of highway, usually on a fishing trip to or from Lake of the Woods, I usually see deer, ruffed or sharp-tail grouse, or a bear. Haglund was hired in 1982 and retired in 2004, and during that time, he cared for that lonely stretch of 72 like it was his own driveway, plowing, scraping, sanding, and salting the highway for maximum safety. "I wanted my road to look good, bare, and dry," Haglund says. "I was concerned about the traveling public."

His truck was a Ford tandem axel truck with ten wheels capable of hauling up to fifty-six thousand pounds of sand and salt. It had a large plow on the front outfitted with a wing plow that directed snow beyond the truck and into the ditch. It also had a scraper blade under the truck, which allowed Haglund to scrape away ice and snow to get to bare asphalt. The truck had six gears and six levers that controlled the equipment. One lever raised and lowered the plow, one raised the dump box with the sand, another two levers controlled the outside wing plows, and two levers operated the underbody scraper, lifting or lowering it and rotating it left to right.

To this day, Haglund can sit in a chair, close his eyes, and reach in midair to where each lever and gear was located in his truck. Like so many drivers, he developed a sixth sense about his truck, knowing instinctively when to raise and lower the plow depending upon the snow's depth and density and how to manipulate the scrape on the pavement to remove troublesome ice. He took pride in knowing how to maneuver the plow and the exploding snow it produced so it wouldn't destroy mailboxes along his route.

"If the mailboxes are set to the correct height, the wing on the plow should slide right underneath them so the snow hits the post and not the box," he says. "I was always pretty concerned about mailboxes. I have one in my own yard, so I made sure I respected the homeowners along my route."

During the worst snowstorms, Haglund's driving abilities kept his snow plow on the road. He said a driver has to constantly be aware of his surroundings, whether of other drivers, mailboxes, or wildlife leaping across the road. His skills were honed during these times to feel the slight slope of the road from the center line to the shoulder beneath the wheels. "There are times when it's white, it looks like you're driving on a field, you can tell there is a 2 percent slope from the middle to the edge of the road, and you can feel that slight tilt in the truck. It's just a little bit of slope," Haglund says. That driving skill helped him negotiate the road during the worst storms. When it got even worse, he would get a call from his supervisor to bring the truck home—it was too bad to even drive the plow.

When a storm struck at night, Haglund would report to work around 3 AM. "If I had an idea that I would be called early, I'd have my lunch already made," he says. "I'd have a quick bowl of oatmeal, and I'd get the call at three o'clock. I'd get to the shop within fifteen minutes or less. Sometimes you'd get a call in the evening, so you want to get the salt and sand on the road so it had some traction." Keeping 72 ice free was Haglund's biggest goal. Some of the ditches were regularly full of water and so deep that if a regular-sized car flipped upside down in it, the car would be virtually invisible under the water.

Drivers pose their own challenges to snowplow truck drivers, and it was Haglund's rule to treat drivers with patience. If a group of cars gathered behind his truck, he would pull to a safe place on the shoulder and let them pass. "I would try to do that every five miles," Haglund said. Predictably, drivers in a rush would pass him on icy roads, and he would come across them a mile or so ahead, their cars in the ditch. Haglund would be sure to call the highway patrol to help them. One mistake drivers make, Haglund says, is driving with the cruise control on when there is heavy snow on the road. When they hit a patch of deep snow, their cars tend to go out of control.

One of the worst storms Haglund experienced occurred in 1997. It rained in the evening and then started to snow, and by the time he got the call to plow, heavy trucks had already been on the highway, packing down the snow and ice into a nearly impenetrable layer. "They had to get the motor graders out to scrape it off," he says.

Over his career, Haglund saw bears, timber wolves, and a lynx cross the road. He sometimes made the fifty-five-mile trip from Baudette to Kelliher three times in a day, racking up more than three hundred miles of snowy driving in a shift. With his plow blade throwing up great gales of snow, Haglund never wavered in his duty. He wanted his road dry.

Pack a Daypack for Summer Hikes

A H, SUMMER. Time to stretch your legs and go for a hike, either along the many state trails (paved or dirt) or perhaps into the backcountry along the Sawtooth Mountains of the North Shore.

I've been on plenty of hikes that went sour after reaching into my backpack and realizing I'd left an essential item at home. Pocketknife for cutting the cheese? Dang it. Mosquito repellant? Double dang.

Here's a checklist for loading your backpack:

» WATER BOTTLE WITH PLENTY OF WATER. Figure on one liter per person for an hour of strenuous hiking.

» MOSQUITO REPELLANT. A small bottle of DEET-based repellant is OK for adults (be sure to read instructions for safe application) and a non-DEET product for children. Our family uses citronella-scented wipes.

» SALVE FOR INSECT BITES. A good product is AfterBite.

» MULTI-TOOL KNIFE. The various tools come in handy whether you need a knife for the cheese or a corkscrew for a bottle.

» A SMALL FIRST-AID KIT. Band-Aids, a tube of antibacterial salve, a small bottle of pain relievers, and any personal medications are a good start.

» LUNCH OR SNACKS. Depending on the length of your hike and your desire to keep your daypack light, you can either have sandwiches, fruit, and wrapped snacks (and a heavier daypack) or pre-wrapped snacks like energy bars.

» A SMALL TABLECLOTH. It's very handy for keeping your meal out of the dirt.

- » COMPASS in case you go off trail.
- » SUNBLOCK.
- » LIGHTWEIGHT RAIN JACKET.
- » MAP if you're taking multiple trails or traveling off trail.
- » CAMERA, although cell phones serve this purpose today.
- » EMERGENCY WHISTLE in case you get lost.

Optional items:
- » Binoculars for spotting wildlife.
- » Guide book for flora, fauna, or both.
- » Lightweight gloves or stocking cap (if you're hiking in the shoulder seasons and expect cool weather).
- » GPS if you're going off trail.
- » Matches or lighter, in case you travel off trail, get lost, and need a fire.
- » Extra lens for camera, such as a telephoto or macro for detailed pictures.

Corn Husk Dolls and Fairy Houses

LIKE MANY FAMILIES, ours looks forward to a meal of sweet corn. When the bag of green, hefty ears lands on the kitchen table, someone has to take it outside and husk each ear. It used to take some cajoling to find a young volunteer for the task, but one day daughter Grace, age eight, disappeared with the corn, brought it back husked, and disappeared again. I found her on the deck with sticks, rubber bands, string, and a glue bottle assembling a corn husk doll. It was something her grandmother from North Carolina had shown her earlier in the summer. That summer, I frequently followed Grace to a shady spot under the pine trees where homemade corn husk dolls and other toys cavorted among invisible fairies. An old birdhouse was turned upside down and made into a fairy house, decorated with natural *objets d'art* like moss and pinecones. "Fairies live in the natural world, so they like things that are made from natural things," Grace said.

A whole world had been created under the pines with objects that adults wouldn't pay much attention to. Here's a bit of how it was done.

Corn Husk Dolls

Carefully remove the husks from the ears of corn, making sure to separate and keep intact the corn silk. Pile the husks in loose stacks and allow them to dry in a place where they won't be disturbed, such as the attic or a sunny windowsill. You can use fresh husks, but any ink applied to them can run.

Corn husk doll

Cut a piece of dowel to six inches or trim a bamboo skewer to the same length. Slip a large bead over the stick and glue it to the end of the stick, like a lollipop. This will be the basis of the doll's head. Cover the bead with one or two husks, bunch the excess husk below the bead, and wrap tightly with light wire or string. Apply a coating of glue if you use string.

For the body, gather a generous wad of husks into a cylinder and bind them at one end with wire or string. Fold the husks over the gather. Lift up the outside husks to expose the inner husks and wrap one string or wire around the gathered outside husks tightly. Slip the stick with the head into the center of the body and push downward. By leaving space between the body and head, you can wrap and glue more husks around the stick and create an abdomen, thus transforming the lower body into a skirt. Insert and glue short pieces of dowel or bamboo skewers into the abdomen for arms.

Fairy Houses

Fairy houses, I discovered one summer, were all over in the woods and in the backyard surrounding our house; I had just never seen them. Some were natural, like a big hole in a pine tree created by a pileated woodpecker; others were created by Grace in case the fairies needed a roadside rest or summer cottage during their travels between some invisible world and ours.

№ **33** **FAST FACTS**

Mud Pies

One summer day, Grace asked her mother to take down from the shelf a thin, tattered book, *Mud Pies and Other Recipes*, printed in 1961, that had belonged to Grace's mother as a child. With book in hand, Grace trotted out to the backyard and worked up a couple of recipes.

LEFT-HANDED MUDLOAF
Sit on the ground with a bowl in front of you full of thick mud. With your left hand, reach out and add a fistful of whatever you find there. Stir and pack into a loaf pan. Mold with left hand.

RIGHT-HANDED MUDLOAF
Follow the recipe for Left-Handed Mudloaf, but this time use your right hand.

DANDELION SOUFFLÉ
After the dandelions in your lawn have gone to seed, shake their fluffy tops into an empty frozen pie pan until it is brimming over. Set in a moderate oven that is out of the wind. While it is cooking, seat your doll at the table located in a light breeze. Serve the soufflé immediately and watch it disappear! You will never have leftovers with this dish.

Fairy house

One fairy house was an old bird-feeder that had fallen out of the tree and lost its plastic sides. It had two walls and a roof. A dried polypore (leathery tree growth) served as a small couch. A seashell was a TV. Some grass clippings were a bed. A pinecone was a Christmas tree (fairies have a different holiday schedule than ours). Some pine needles made for nice soft carpeting. A dandelion flower was, well, a dandelion flower for decoration. Another fairy house, a garden cottage, was located near the flower garden wall. Four sticks kept aloft a roof of soft moss. Some immature carrots (borrowed from the family garden) were planted in front along with a few cherry tomatoes, which in the fairy world were quite large and delicious meals. The cottage walls were leaves from nearby bee balm plants, giving the hut a nice aroma. A few dandelion leaves were rows of lettuce.

The planning, design, and interior decoration of these fairy homes kept Grace busy for several summer days. The garden cottage soon wilted and disappeared, but she returned to the birdfeeder cottage the following summer and elevated it into the crook of a tree, which, with her father's help, became a fairy tree house. The furnishings changed almost daily, as rocks, sticks, leaves, acorns, and other natural materials rotated through the house as various decorations and furniture.

The visiting fairies, I was told, were very grateful for the accommodations.

The Basics of Bird-Watching

BIRD-WATCHING SUFFERS from a nerdy reputation. Think of bird-watchers, and you conjure up a middle-aged man in khaki shorts and shirt, multi-pocketed vest, and binoculars hanging around his neck. I am not that person, though I am an avid bird-watcher.

In fact, everyone in my immediate family is a bird-watcher. Our family keeps a birdfeeder on the rail of our deck and a pair of binoculars next to the kitchen table. We're backyard bird-watchers, and there are millions like us in cities and in rural areas. I see lots of interesting birds while in the woods and on the prairies, but my most rewarding bird-watching experiences are right outside my dining room window.

Over the years, we've added hummingbird feeders, bluebird houses, and wood duck nesting boxes to our backyard in order to bring us closer to those species. More importantly, we've kept our backyard in a mostly natural state to provide bird-attracting habitat. We keep a few dead trees for perching sites for the swallows and the great horned owl in our neighborhood, and we don't cut the strip of cattails along our backyard marsh. We know the marsh is an important breeding and nesting area for red-winged blackbirds. We keep some underbrush uncut for the gray catbirds on the edges of our yard because we like to hear their plaintive, meowlike calls.

To see birds, we provide them with habitat and some food at our feeders, and this gives us a lot of joy. Urban dwellers don't need a marsh nearby; some easy landscaping with bird-friendly plants for food and nesting can certainly draw birds to your home.

In addition to backyard viewing, there is a whole other world of bird-watching. That is the active method, identifying and noting the populations of birds while you're out hiking, camping, fishing, cycling, or spending a day at the cabin. Because birds are all around us in the outdoors, bird-watching is an easy sport to enjoy. Their world is readily available for us to learn and understand.

What You'll Need

» BINOCULARS. We own three pairs of binoculars and none are terribly expensive, but they are critical to getting a good look at birds for proper identification. We keep an inexpensive pair by the dining room table so we can quickly look at what might be perched at our birdfeeder or flitting about in our backyard. They cost about $100, and they get a fair amount of abuse from the kids and their friends because we make them readily accessible. I wouldn't put out a pair of $600 binoculars for that reason.

I own two pairs of more expensive binoculars ($200 to $500). One pair I keep in my vehicle, and another I keep handy just for hunting and bird-watching trips. If you are able to give them proper care, a pair of high-end binoculars is a worthy investment. You'll be impressed by the superior optics and ease with which you're able to see a junco in thick brush. There are many excellent evaluations of binoculars on the Internet and at retailers. Do your homework and invest in a pair.

» A GUIDEBOOK. The beauty of bird-watching is discovering what you're looking at. One spring morning, a handsome, small bird was chirping from the underbrush near a creek by my house. I was bothered that I didn't know what it was. When I got home, I grabbed my bird guide and discovered it was a male ruby-crowned kinglet; it perfectly resembled the picture in the book. It gave me great satisfaction to find out that the little red-feathered crown on its head goes up and down when the males are excited—a behavior I had observed that morning—and a courtship display was under way. After consulting my guidebook further, I returned to the creek and discovered several male and female kinglets feeding and trying to impress each other. My day was made complete by this small discovery in the bird world.

An excellent guide is *The Sibley Guide to Birds,* by David Allen Sibley, and the companion guide, *The Sibley Guide to Bird Life and Behavior.* These guides sit on the bookshelf near our dining room table and get used frequently.

» Cʟᴏᴛʜɪɴɢ. Sure, you can buy the multi-pocket vest, but the best clothing is whatever is suitable for the season. Layering is a good way to stay warm during the early spring, late fall, and winter months. A ball cap can block the sun and improve your vision. I prefer to dress in drab colors (camouflage is ideal if you truly want to get close to birds) and wear comfortable shoes, light hiking boots, or even waders, depending upon the environment. Unless it is hunting season, when blaze orange is in order, brightly colored clothing only serves to alert birds to your presence.

Understanding Habitat

Bird guides can help you understand what birds occupy different habitats, which is important to know if you're actively looking for birds. On a hike in a pine forest, you'll see much different species than if you're walking near a marsh or through a mixed hardwood forest. When I'm running near open fields or edges of hardwood forests, I'll be on the lookout for bluebirds. Walking along a marsh, I'll be watching for shorebirds, waterfowl, and raptors that hunt along marshlands. Careful observation and understanding of habitat is helpful in identifying the birds you see. If you have little habitat in your backyard, you can improve it by planting flowers, trees, and fruit-bearing shrubs that will attract different types of birds. There are many helpful landscaping guides for attracting birds.

Seasons

It is important to understand how the seasons affect birds and what species you see. Spring is the season of bounty for bird-watchers; many species that may not normally inhabit your neighborhood may pass through during their northward migration. I'm always watching for species of ducks that nest in northern Minnesota and Canada (lesser scaup, for instance) but will stop and rest in southern areas during their spring migration.

Of course, many species leave Minnesota in the fall and winter, but the latter is one of the best times to see assorted species of owls, such as great gray owls, that migrate to the state in the winter months. Fall and spring are good times to see migrating birds of prey, especially along the North Shore; it is easier to spot them when there is little foliage in the woods. Large concentrations of loons are often seen in late fall as they prepare to migrate south. Mornings and evenings are usually the best times to see birds as they feed or engage in breeding displays.

Where to Go

Minnesota has plenty of public lands that are havens for wild birds. State parks have a variety of different habitats, and that diversity, along with their mix of locations around the state, makes them good places for bird-watching. Each park has its own birding list compiled by experts. State and county parks provide bird-watching opportunities, but some urban parks are so well manicured that prime wildlife habitat can be scarce.

Wildlife Management Areas are state-owned lands managed by the Department of Natural Resources. Big and small, Wildlife Management Areas are spread across the state, are open to the public, and often have excellent diversity of habitat for attracting birds. At more than thirty thousand acres of diverse wetland and upland habitat, the Carlos Avery Wildlife Management Area near Forest Lake is a hot spot for Twin Cities birders.

Waterfowl Production Areas are common throughout western and southwestern Minnesota. They are owned by the U.S. Fish and Wildlife Service and were purchased with migratory waterfowl stamp revenue. With both wetlands and uplands, National Wildlife Refuges are excellent areas for bird-watching and sometimes have birding trails and printed guides.

Minnesota is blessed with two national forests, the Chippewa and Superior, which provide ample bird-watching opportunities in the north-central and northeastern parts of the state. State forests, like national forests, attract an abundance of woodland birds. Information on all these areas can be found easily on the Internet.

Know Your Bait

Night Crawlers

The do-all bait, night crawlers can catch everything from walleyes to brown trout. Bait stores sell them in foam containers, or you can collect them yourself during rainy nights or in the morning after a summer storm. There are several ways of hooking them. You can thread a single hook through the tip or "nose" of the night crawler; this simple method is often used to catch trout, bass, and walleye. There are also crawler rigs that have several hooks (two to three) that are tied to a piece of monofilament line. One hook is threaded through the crawler's nose and another through the mid-section. If there is a third hook, it is attached to the rear of the night crawler. The crawler rig is used mainly for trolling and often has several colorful beads and spinners in front of the hooks that provide extra movement and attraction to fish. While anglers used to harvest their own night crawlers regularly, the practice is less popular since night crawlers are so ubiquitous in bait and tackle stores and are inexpensive, usually $2.50 to $4 a dozen.

Leeches

Ribbon leeches have been called "black gold" in the bait business because they fetch high prices and are typically in high demand by anglers. Bait dealers harvest leeches from shallow ponds or lakes using baited mesh leech traps. They are sorted by size, kept in cold water, and sold by the dozen or by the pound. Anglers usually buy them in shallow plastic containers with lids; without the lid, leeches quickly escape, a habit not unnoticed by the unwary angler who hasn't secured the container. Ribbon leeches shouldn't be confused with horse leeches, known commonly as blood suckers. Ribbon leeches will briefly attach to your finger as you try to put them on a hook—a habit that leaves some novice (and squeamish) anglers a bit unsettled—but with a firm grip, you can usually wrangle a leech onto a hook without much trouble. A leech is hooked through its largest firm and fleshy sucker mouth. Small leeches fished under a bobber are excellent bait for bluegills and are commonly slowly trolled on a long monofilament rig for walleyes. Walleyes are, in fact, voracious consumers of bottom-dwelling aquatic insects, and a ribbon leech is usually too good for them to pass up.

Leaf or Red Worms

These small, pink- to red-colored worms are commonly used for panfish. Night crawlers have over the years become more popular than leaf worms, but anglers of bluegills and trout swear by them. They are usually threaded two or three times on a hook and fished beneath a bobber.

Spikes

These multicolored "worms" are actually maggots, usually from the blow or blue-bottle fly. Commercial raisers of spikes can turn them blue, red, or yellow by applying different dyes to their food (usually some meat product). Anglers tend to believe these different colors catch more fish, and on days when fish are finicky, that might be true. Spikes, along with waxworms, are exclusively used for panfish like bluegills, crappies, and pumpkinseed.

Waxworms

Minnesota's most popular bait for panfish, waxworms are the larvae of bee or wax moths. Bait stores sell them in small, opaque containers with a small amount of sawdust for bedding. Waxworms are fat and, well, juicy, which might explain the attraction to bluegills and crappies. They are usually threaded on a hook one or two at a time and fished below a bobber. Waxworms are raised in large warehouses and can be purchased in bulk.

Fathead Minnow

The do-all minnow in Minnesota, the fathead is hardy, and it appeals to a wide variety of game fish. They are typically sold in lengths from two to three inches; the smallest fatheads are sold under the name "crappie minnows." A study in the 1990s estimated the sales of fathead minnows in Minnesota at $34 million. Fatheads are easily the least expensive of bait minnows. Anglers usually buy them from dealers in an oxygen-filled plastic bag with water and transport the minnows that way until they are ready to put them in a minnow bucket. Fatheads are threaded on the hook either through the snout or just under the dorsal fin. A fathead minnow on a small, lead-headed jig has probably caught more walleyes in Minnesota than any other method.

White Sucker

White suckers are the bratwurst of bait. Large and tough, white suckers are among the most common fish in Minnesota; for that reason, they are also a common prey for many large game fish. While they can reach up to five pounds, most white suckers that are sold weigh a few ounces to a half pound and are four to ten inches long. They're also called pike minnows because they're commonly used to catch northern pike. White suckers are usually hooked once under the dorsal fin and fished beneath a bobber or, in the winter, used under a tip-up, an ice-fishing contraption that raises a red flag when a fish bites.

Redtail Chub

The redtail chub is actually a hornyhead chub, but anglers and bait dealers call them redtails. They are commonly sold in central Minnesota for walleye fishing. Some anglers will catch redtails in streams on very light tackle.

Spottail Shiner

Probably the most coveted baitfish, spottails fetch a premium price in bait shops and are typically available for a short period in the spring. They're a favorite minnow for walleye anglers and are fished using similar techniques as fatheads.

Winter Car Survival and Functions

WINTER DRIVING IS A SKILL. It takes preparation, behind-the-wheel acumen, patience, and maybe a bit of grit. Grit? If you get stranded on a prairie road during a snowstorm, the Minnesota Department of Public Safety urges you to stay put and put your survival instincts to work. "Don't expect to be comfortable," the department states in its public information material. "The challenge is to survive until you're found."

That Emergency Car Kit

Whether you should carry an emergency car kit in your vehicle is debatable. Most don't, believing that their cell phone will help them out of trouble if they become stranded. But during large, freeway-closing snowstorms, there comes the inevitable story of a motorist who makes a bad decision, becomes stranded in a remote area, and has to await help. Here's what Minnesota's Division of Homeland Security and Emergency Management recommends for your car emergency kit:

》 Three-pound coffee can, candle stubs, and matches, which can be used to melt snow for additional drinking water; metal or plastic cup

》 Red bandanna and a plastic whistle to alert rescuers to your location

》 Pencil and paper

》 First-aid kit, including any essential medications

》 Plastic flashlight with spare batteries (Reverse the batteries to avoid accidental switching and burnout, and replace batteries yearly.)

》 Two large plastic garbage bags and safety pins (Bags are for insulation for feet, safety pins keep the bags together.)

》 Snack foods for energy, such as candy bars

》 Gloves or mittens, winter boots, a blanket and/or sleeping bag, jumper cables, a basic toolbox, shovel, bag of sand or other grit for traction, tow cable or chain, road flares and reflectors. You could also consider an extra set of dry clothing or a snowmobile suit.

》 The agency also warns that if you become stranded, never leave your vehicle. Your chances of survival greatly increase if you stay put.

OTHER STRANDED MOTORIST SURVIVAL TIPS

Stay calm and don't exert yourself so much that you get excessively sweaty; wet clothing loses insulation value. Keep fresh air in your vehicle. Don't run the engine unless you're sure the exhaust pipe is snow free. Loosen tight clothing to increase blood circulation, huddle close to others to stay warm, and rub hands together to stay warm. To keep from draining your battery, use emergency flashers only if you hear an approaching vehicle. Always keep one person awake and alert to watch for other vehicles or your rescuers.

CELLULAR PHONE USERS

You can call 511 statewide twenty-four hours a day to get up-to-date road and weather conditions, road construction reports, and other traffic information. You access the same information via the Internet at www.511mn.org.

Driving Skills

The Minnesota Department of Transportation offers these winter driving tips:

» Minnesota law requires drivers to use headlights when it is snowing or sleeting.

» Keep snow and ice from vehicle hood, windows, headlights, brake lights, and directional signals.

» In extreme weather conditions, don't travel unless absolutely necessary. Tell others of your travel plans and arrival times. Carry a cell phone, but don't use it while driving. Also, if you're stranded, your cell phone can alert others to your location, but use it tactically to save battery time.

» Adjust your driving speed to road and weather conditions. Drive slower, and you'll lower your chances of a crash. Don't use cruise control on snow-covered roads.

» Move over one lane from any stopped emergency vehicle.

» Keep a safe stopping distance between vehicles, and leave extra room between your vehicle and snowplows. Drive defensively.

» Be familiar with how your brakes react on snow-covered roads.

How to Jump a Dead Battery with Another Car

Park cars close together, and make sure they are not touching. Turn off ignitions and put them either in park or neutral (depending on whether you have a manual or automatic transmission). Turn off any accessory lights and radio.

Pick out the positive (red) end of one jumper cable and attach it to the positive (indicated by the +) post on the dead battery. Make sure the clamp is tight. Attach the other positive cable end to the positive post of the good battery. If terminals are corroded, you might have to scrape them to get a good connection.

Attach the negative (black) cable to the good battery's negative (indicated by the –) post. Now attach the other end of the negative cable to an unpainted bolt or bracket on the dead car, making sure it's away from the dead battery.

Make sure the cables aren't close to any moving parts or belts. Start the good battery car and run it for a few minutes. Now start the dead vehicle and let both vehicles idle. If the dead car doesn't start, recheck cables for the proper connections. If the dead car still won't start, check for other malfunctions.

Remove cables in reverse order. If the battery is in poor condition, it might have to be jumped again. If you have doubts, make sure you drive your car to a repair shop or where you're assured of getting another jump.

How to Inline Skate and Waterski

Two favorite summertime sports—inline skating and waterskiing—have their roots in Minnesota. Both were started by tinkers, both became sporting sensations, and both remain popular today with many offshoots into racing, trick performances, and youth-oriented subcultures.

Inline Skating

Inspired by an old skate found in a rummage store, hockey-playing brothers Scott and Brennan Olson of Minneapolis put polyurethane rollers on a hockey skate and started a sporting craze.

The brothers founded the company Rollerblade in their parents' basement. While the concept of an inline skate had been around for about one hundred years, Rollerblade's popularity made its trademarked name synonymous with the sport. The Olsons eventually sold the company to investors, and Rollerblade, with many product competitors today, is owned by the Italian company Tecnica Group S.p.A, which also owns the Nordica ski boot company.

Inline skating involves the same movements as ice skating. To start, make sure your skates fit well; they should be snug fitting with no sloppiness. Make sure you have the proper safety gear, such as a helmet, knee and elbow pads, wrist guards, and gloves. Hitting the pavement at a good clip creates something called road rash. And broken bones, sometimes. Safety gear is critical for inline skating.

Begin practice on a flat piece of concrete or pavement that is edged by grass. You can also start indoors on carpet, but it's a little difficult to get any speed. Put on your skates in the grass (or on carpet), stand up, and try taking a few small steps. Start slowly with small steps and then try walking. The idea is to balance on the skates and get used to the sensation of rolling.

Next, move to a hard surface, where you will roll more easily. Try not to stand up straight; bend your knees, keep your hands in front of you, and keep your feet in a V-shaped stance. Once you start moving on a hard surface, you'll experience the "duck walk." When you step, you'll glide a bit. This is a good thing.

Once you're moving and gliding, try using the brake mounted on the back of the skate. Apply the brake by pressing it toward the surface. Practice this a lot. If you fall, be sure to fall on your pads, not on your tailbone. Always begin your practices on a flat surface until you've mastered your brake, turning, and speed control. One of the biggest mistakes beginners make is hitting the hills too soon. Also, taking lessons, either from a friend or instructor, is a good idea.

Waterskiing: Its Earliest Roots

Ralph Samuelson was a pretty amazing and inventive guy. In 1922 he dreamed he could "ski" on the water. He tried putting barrel staves on his feet and getting pulled by a boat. It didn't work. He switched the staves to snow skis, but they didn't work well either. He finally fashioned a pair of extra-wide boards with straps to keep them on his feet. Holding a hundred-foot-long sash cord attached to the back of a boat, Samuelson ordered his brother to tow him at twenty miles per hour. The sport of waterskiing was born on Lake Pepin, a wide spot in the Mississippi River, in Lake City, Minnesota. Samuelson went on to demonstrate the new sport around the country for the next fifteen years. A plaque along the shore of Lake Pepin commemorates his achievement.

Today's waterskiers benefit from faster boats and better skis than those at Samuelson's disposal, but the essence of being pulled across the water by a boat hasn't changed. The three most important things to remember in water skiing are: keep your knees bent, back straight, and arms extended.

Let's back up a bit. Before you jump in the water, you'll need a Coast Guard–approved life jacket that fits properly. Be sure to read the label to make sure it's the proper size; don't take a chance on an old or ill-fitting life jacket. Also, read up on Minnesota's waterskiing laws, gathered in the Department of Natural Resources' water and boating safety guide. It's online and available at marine and boat retailers and from the DNR.

Ralph Samuelson, inventor of waterskiing, took adventure one step further: in 1925, he was pulled by a World War I Curtis Flying Boat that allowed him to jump over five-foot floats.

Adjust the bindings on your skis so they snugly fit your feet. It's best to do this out of the water. Put your skis on, either in the water or on the boat's swim platform if it has one.

Lie on your back with the rope handle in front of you and the rope between your knees and skis. Grab the handle with your legs fully bent toward your chest, your arms extended, and your elbows outside your knees. You should be positioned like you're curled into a ball. Be sure the skis are pointed toward the boat, their tips above the water, about shoulder wide.

Motion the driver to take up the slack in the rope. Once the slack is out, tell the driver to go. (Some skiers say "Hit it!" but you can say whatever you want.) Once you're moving forward, you'll want to immediately straighten your knees, but wait for the boat to go fast enough to pull you over the plane of the water. Stay in the curled/sitting position for about four to five seconds, and then push up with both legs and stand.

Keep in mind your knees are shock absorbers, so keep them bent to absorb any waves. Also, keep your back straight and don't bend over at your waist. Keep the rope extended in front of you so you can pull it toward you in case any slack appears. If you're a beginner, start easy. Waterskiing can be punishing to your legs and arms, especially if you fall a lot. As with inline skating, it helps to take lessons from a friend or instructor.

Summer Beach and Woods Fun

S O IT IS A SUMMER DAY, and you hear the familiar refrain "I'm bored" from a youngster. Or worse yet, the plea for "something to do" is a chorus coming from a clan of impatient, shorts-wearing youngsters. What to do?

Bryan Atchison is a professional summer funmeister. He is a summer camp counselor for the YMCA Twin Cities. "I work at three different camps and consult at five others," he says. Atchison spends his summer days outdoors in the company of lots of excitable, imaginative children, yet his methods for engaging them don't include lots of expensive playground equipment or sophisticated toys. He lets nature and imagination be his guides. He also relies heavily on the fact that kids like to play with adults who share their imaginations. "If it's something that involves a lot of props or more than one ball, chances are we aren't going to do it," he says. "Activities always last long longer if an adult is there sharing in the fun."

So how does he do it?

Sand Castles
A lake beach and wet sand is a recipe for hours of imaginative play, Atchison says. Luckily many YMCA camps are located on lakes with plenty of sandy beaches. Armed with legions of sour cream tubs and ice cream buckets, counselors and campers

descend on the beach for "build offs," where groups split up and try to build the most creative and towering sand castles. "It ignites imagination and keeps you outside in the sunshine," Atchison says. Piles of sand are transformed into walls, towers, bridges, jails, and moats. Sticks, shells, and rocks are incorporated into the castles as decoration and architectural support. Once the creations are completed, a "celebrity" lifeguard may judge them. "It doesn't matter whether you have three kids or fifty kids—it's a successful project. You just build. Our biggest thing is the counselor there building, too, not just watching."

Creative Canoeing

Children and adults view canoeing differently, Atchison says. Adults enjoy the quiet time on the water, no doubt happy to be away from the responsibilities of adult life. Children, however, can get impatient with canoeing, so Atchison and his counselors turn canoe trips into grand adventures. A destination is always involved, usually a nearby island that has a magical story. One camp has an island called Alligator Island that involves a long story about an alligator that becomes transported to the lake during a flood. Another island has imaginary trap doors with access to unusual places. "You knock on the trap door, and a restaurant gives you a French fry," Atchison says. Of course, it's imaginary, and the canoeing adventures are built around stories and tales passed down each summer from counselors. Campers become imbued in the fabric of island storytelling and the traditions of each camp. And they're inspired to keep on paddling.

Fort Building

No hammers, nails, or bolts are needed. Atchison will lead a troupe of youngsters into a camp forest where the only building supplies are cut tree branches and sticks. Building a fort begins by leaning one long branch against a tree. Once you have this roof branch, you can begin piling additional branches against it for walls. "You make a teepee against the tree," Atchison says. Tunnels can be created by leaning tree boughs against each other. A floor can be swept away with a broom. Rooms can be added with additional branches and scrap wood. An old bed sheet comes in handy for a roof. "Forts are cool," Atchison says. "We build a lot of forts at camp, and we let some of them stay for a few weeks." The best part about forts is they can be torn down and redesigned by different creative minds. And they are biodegradable.

Ice Dam Confidential

IN THE WINTER OF 2010–11, Minnesotans had a bad case of the ice dams. Record snow piled up in December, catching homeowners off guard as their roof edges began to grow the dreaded chunks of ice, the working front edge of a roof disaster. By midwinter, mild concern blossomed into freak-out as dammed roof water manifested on leaky ceilings. Contractors were suddenly raking in the cash by raking off roofs and using steam and salt to remove dams. The popular saying that Minnesota has two seasons, winter and road construction, grew a corollary: ice dam season was the new winter. The heck with road construction.

I was one of the freaking-out homeowners. My ice dams seemingly grew overnight. I spent an entire weekend shoveling the snow off my roof, only to do it again a few weeks later. I chipped at the ice dams, applied calcium chloride to melt them away, and shoveled and shoveled. By the end of winter, the piles of ice and snow around my house were so high, our Labrador would walk past the kitchen window and all I could see were her ankles.

Along the way, I learned a few things about the rooftop scourge.

Ice dams are often a home insulation problem. While a lot of snow on the roof is the beginning of ice dam problems, the real issue is the melting of the snow, usually at quick pace, and the water that runs down the roof and freezes when it reaches the

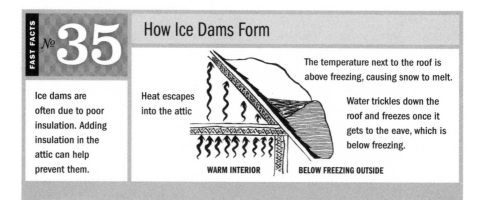

FAST FACTS

№ **35**

How Ice Dams Form

Ice dams are often due to poor insulation. Adding insulation in the attic can help prevent them.

Heat escapes into the attic

The temperature next to the roof is above freezing, causing snow to melt.

Water trickles down the roof and freezes once it gets to the eave, which is below freezing.

WARM INTERIOR　**BELOW FREEZING OUTSIDE**

roof edge. Poor attic insulation allows warm inside air to reach the roof, melting the snow. Warm air leakage can also come from exhaust fans in the kitchen or bathroom that transfer heat into the attic. In my situation, ice dams form in two locations on the roof: around the bathroom exhaust fan and the chimney. They were also where I had some thin insulation in my attic, I later discovered.

THE LONG-TERM FIX. A good strategy to avoid winter ice dams is to improve your attic insulation and fix any warm air leaking into the attic space. In my case, I fixed the gap around the bathroom exhaust fan where it leaked warm air into the attic. Homeowners should also look for other areas in their ceilings where warm-air leakage is a problem, such as around recessed ceiling lights, heating ducts, and skylights.

I also purchased some extra insulation batts and placed them in the attic where I noticed there was little snow on the roof. A good home contractor can examine your attic insulation and identify and fix any deficiencies. Improving your attic insulation is also a good way to lower your energy bill.

THE SHORT-TERM FIX. The obvious short-term fix is to remove snow from your roof. It eliminates the key ingredient—water—that will create an ice dam. You can use a roof rake or broom, but it is crucial that you don't damage shingles or other roof materials, or you may be compounding your problem. Some experts suggest not scraping off snow down to the roof, but leaving an inch of snow. If your ice dam is creating water problems inside your house, you need to make channels in the dam to drain away the water collecting behind it. One remedy is to fill panty hose with calcium chloride and lay the tube across the ice dam and slightly over the edge of the roof. The de-icing tube will melt a channel through the dam, but it is important that it lays over the edge of the roof so water can drain away.

The Essential Elements of a Rope Swing

ROPE SWINGS ARE the perfect place to spend a summer day, whether you swing over a favorite swimming hole or in the backyard while being pushed by a parent. Single rope swings can be hung using items bought from the lumberyard or hardware store. There are three basic components: the seat, the rope, and hardware needed to hang it.

SEAT. I built our backyard rope swing with a seat made of a chunk of two-by-six-by-sixteen-inch cedar board, but you can also make a seat by gluing two pieces of wood together for a wider platform. The seat can be either rectangular or circular. It can be painted or left with raw wood. I prefer cedar because it weathers the harsh Minnesota elements well. Once you've built or selected a board for your swing, drill a one-inch-diameter hole in the middle. It's important the hole is squarely in the middle for a well-balanced seat.

HANGING ROPE. Purchase the appropriate length of rope for your swing. Measure the height of the swing, but be sure to add enough rope length for several knots. Accurate measuring is critical because when you purchase your rope, the clerk will cut it to length. You can learn a lot about rope strengths online. I purchased a three-quarter-inch, three-strand polyester rope because it is resistant to rot and ultraviolet light and ages well. It's important to use rope that will survive in the elements. Note, too, that some varieties of rope will stretch more than others. Any home improvement or hardware store clerk can help you with the rope selection.

My rope is wrapped around a stout branch and tied with a knot, and it has held up well for five years, but some homeowners suggest drilling a hole through the branch and installing an eye-bolt through the hole, to which the rope is attached. In the long run, either method may damage the tree limb, but trees can typically survive a hole drilled through a branch, whereas a rope around a branch can continually damage the bark. If you install the eye-bolt through the branch, you can attach a metal thimble (a kind of oval metal ring) at the end of the rope to reduce friction on the rope and then attach the thimble to the eye-bolt with a closeable carbiner or spring-loaded hook.

INSTALLING THE SEAT. Once the top end of the rope is attached to the tree, the bottom, or tag end, is threaded through the hole in the seat. Tie a knot or two below the seat to hold it in place. Adjust the knot's height according to the height of the children using the swing.

MAINTENANCE. Be sure to regularly check the rope for abrasions, rot, and other damage that might weaken it. Check the branch, too, to make sure it is retaining its strength. A cracked or damaged seat should be replaced.

Getting Lost and Getting Found

To the inexperienced adventurer, Minnesota's backcountry might not seem dangerous or wild. Many places are crisscrossed by remote roads and trails, and even the Boundary Waters gets busy in the summer. How hard could it be to get lost or, worse yet, die?

Actually, not hard, and there are plenty of stories of hunters, backpackers, and other adventurers who get lost in the swamps and dense forests. Some are found, some die, and some are never seen again. Lacking in elevation, Minnesota's woods don't offer lost souls many visible landmarks. Combined with plenty of opportunities to get wet by falling in marshes or bogs and the vagaries of weather, it's easy to see how getting lost could quickly become disastrous. While county sheriff departments, with access to volunteer search-and-rescue squads and state helicopters, are well skilled and equipped to find lost people, the task is made more difficult by the same things that lead people to get lost: vast tracks of forests and cold and wet weather. Throw in the difficulty of night search and rescue, and the challenge of locating lost people increases. Thus, the rule of thumb is: be prepared. A few other tips also help:

Map and compass. Don't venture into the woods without a map and compass. Many hikes have turned disastrous or near disastrous by hikers or hunters who assumed they knew where they were and where they were going. In this era of Global Positioning System (GPS) and Google Earth, knowing where you are is, electronically speaking, not difficult. But that makes several assumptions: your GPS won't lose battery power, and you've thought to print out a map and carry it. Sometimes it is as simple as picking up a trail map of the area at a trailhead or putting a compass in your pocket as you head out in search of grouse. A compass doesn't require batteries and fits easily in your pocket. It has saved its share of lives.

Tell someone where you are going. As Aron Ralston so famously demonstrated in the movie *127 Hours,* even the best-prepared and experienced adventurers don't prepare enough. In Ralston's case, it meant cutting off his arm in a Utah canyon when he became inexorably wedged between rocks. His chief mistake: he never told anyone where he was headed, assuming he wouldn't need to be rescued. It is the number-one warning search and rescuers give to would-be lost adventurers hoping to be found: if no one knows the general location where you were headed, chances that you'll be found decrease considerably. In many cases, so little is known about a lost person's destination that search efforts are the proverbial needle in a haystack.

EQUIPMENT AND SUPPLIES. Bring along basic survival equipment and dress for the weather. A pack of matches, flashlight, and whistle easily fit into a pocket or backpack, and they can mean the difference in survival. Extra water and food, such as energy bars or candy, have saved many lives as well. Many adventurers fail to anticipate weather conditions and don't bring adequate clothing. Without a rain jacket, a lost person will face a high probability of chill and hypothermia even if temperatures are moderate. One of the best items to head off the cold is a stocking cap, and it's easy to put in a backpack. First-aid kits these days are more sophisticated and compact than ever. They are essential equipment, even for short trips.

DON'T TRAVEL ALONE. The lure of solo adventure is powerful, but it also decreases the odds of survival if something goes horribly wrong. Search and rescuers urge lost groups to stay together. Groups can be emotionally fragile, but they can also reach sensible decisions that can help in rescue events. Splitting up also means rescuers have to look in many locations for separate individuals at the same time. Medical emergencies are easier to deal with when two people are working together. The solo adventurer is left to his or her own skills in a medical emergency.

SIGNALS. Be prepared to signal your potential rescuers. Cell phones are handy in a pinch; lost people have often used them to give descriptions of their locations to rescuers, and in some cases, the cell signal can be used to help locate the caller. But over time, cell phones lose battery power and are rendered useless; moreover, some remote areas don't have reliable service. That is why fires and whistles are useful to signal your location when electronic devices fail. Brightly colored clothing is helpful, too. Some expedition canoeists make sure to bring brightly colored life jackets, rain gear, or tarps for signaling purposes.

Foraging: Wild Foods from the Woods

WITH A NEW INTEREST in wild foods thanks to the locavore movement, wild food foraging is gaining popularity. However, there has always been a group of folks who collect mushrooms and wild berries. A trip to the Boundary Waters in August is sure to yield wild blueberries for pancakes, while May is always the month that morel mushroom enthusiasts circle on their calendar.

Wild Fruit

WILD BLUEBERRIES. These berries have been on my foraging menu since childhood. One of my earliest memories is picking blueberries with my grandmother in Itasca County and asking her to repeat over and over the story of her meeting a black bear in the blueberry bog. Years later, I was driving near Finland, Minnesota, one summer afternoon and noticed a wealth of blueberry bushes along the national forest road. I stopped and discovered one of the thickest patches of pinky-finger-sized berries I'd ever seen. I was headed to Ely, but the rest of the day's schedule was thrown out the window as I grabbed whatever containers I had in the vehicle and picked blueberries until dark.

FAST FACTS

№ **36**

Native Wild Blueberries

There are two varieties of native wild blueberries in Minnesota— the sweet lowbush blueberry and the velvet leaf blueberry. The lowbush has very small serrations along its leaf edges, and the velvet leaf has soft, tiny hairs on its leaves, as its name suggests. The species sometimes grow side by side. Shrub and tree expert Welby R. Smith, author of the authoritative *Trees and Shrubs of Minnesota*, says both plants produce tasty, edible berries, and "most berry pickers do not distinguish between the two."

Wild blueberries are common in the forested regions of northern Minnesota, especially in the Arrowhead and border region. They are often found in dry sandy soil near pine trees. I'm regularly surprised to see how little forest soil is required to sustain blueberries when I find them along exposed ridges in the Boundary Waters. They also thrive in an opposite environment: low-lying sphagnum bogs. Blueberries prefer soil that is acidic, which explains their abundance near pines and in bogs. Bushes are low and rarely reach above your knee. Leaves are small, long, and elliptical; once you learn to identify them, they are easily spotted along the ground cover. The plants themselves are twiggy and sometimes sparse in foliage, but they form colonies, and once you find one plant, you'll often find yourself in blueberry heaven. Plants flower in June and produce fruit in late July though August.

Blueberry plants thrive in landscapes burned by wildfires, and if you're serious about picking a lot of berries, you should focus your efforts in fire-ravaged areas of the northland. Recent major forest fires like the Cavity Lake and Ham Lake Fires in the Boundary Waters have been a boon to blueberry production. Wilderness travelers in the region scarred by the Pagami Creek Fire (2011) should bring their blueberry buckets.

Like many wild foods, blueberries require favorable weather conditions and environments. Blueberries seem to need the right amounts of rainfall at the right times for maximum production. I've heard pickers predict a bountiful harvest early in the summer, only to be disappointed when hot, dry weather withers berries in July and August. While blueberries are shade tolerant in bogs, I've often found the biggest and best blueberries on edges of bog openings where berries get the right mix of sunshine and shade.

Shallow buckets are best for picking berries. While sturdy, blueberries can get crushed if you don't distribute them evenly in your picking container. In a rush, I've picked berries and put them in bags, only to find the ones on the bottom turned into pulp.

WILD RASPBERRIES. Returning from a fishing trip to Leech Lake one summer afternoon, I decided to turn down a dirt forest road and try some berry picking. The vague outline of a logging road caught my eye, and I stopped to investigate. It was mid-August, and mosquitoes were sparse, save for shady areas, and I quickly caught sight of wild raspberry bushes lining the trail. Their full, red berries stood out in the sunshine, and I returned to the truck for a bucket. (It's a good idea to keep a berry-picking bucket in your vehicle any time you're traveling in northern Minnesota in August.) The trail was ideal wild raspberry habitat—a mix of full sunlight and shade along the edge of a forest cutting. As I followed the road, the raspberries were more abundant, and I became aware that I wasn't the first to discover the patch. Some of the bushes had recently been crushed by a bear, which left a few strands of black hair on the bushes.

Wild raspberries grow on medium-sized bushes with straight canes with serrated, elliptical leaves. Wild raspberries are fairly common throughout the state, but I've had the most success finding them in north-central Minnesota. The berries appear in July through August, and you can often pick both wild raspberries and blueberries on the same trip. Wild raspberries are more fragile than blueberries, so be careful to use a shallow bucket and to not pile berries excessively deep, or they will get crushed.

Wild Veggies

WILD LEEKS OR RAMPS. This springtime plant, a member of the genus *Allium*, grows throughout the state in partially shaded forests. They grow in colonies of eight- to twelve-inch plants that form a thick ground cover. When you crush their waxy leaves, they give off a pungent, onion-like aroma. They also are identified by their long oval and pointed leaves. The late wild foods expert Gil Quaal of Deer River was an ardent fan of wild leeks, also called ramps, and he once took me to one of his favorite spots and filled a bucket with them. The lower leaves and bulbs are substituted for onions, yellow or green, in soups and other dishes. They can also be eaten raw. Their onion flavor is punctuated with a garlicky taste that adds a different element to dishes.

WATERCRESS. Watercress grows alongside of and in shallow streams, particularly in southeastern Minnesota. It can be eaten raw or steamed and has a peppery taste. It's not advised to harvest watercress from streams where livestock may have polluted the water with dung and urine.

FIDDLEHEADS. The tender, coiled tips of ostrich ferns look like the ends of a violin. A very large fern, the ostrich is found throughout Minnesota. The tips are encased in an onionskin covering, which should not detract from their appeal as a wild edible. They can be eaten fresh or sautéed like asparagus. Don't confuse them with the bracken fern, which also has springtime fiddleheads but that experts have warned is carcinogenic. How do you identify an ostrich fern fiddlehead? It will have a light brown, paperlike parchment covering the fiddlehead, and the stalk will have a smooth, not fuzzy, texture under the parchment. The most distinctive characteristic of ostrich fern fiddleheads is the deep U-shaped groove in the stem; other fern fiddleheads stems are round and have a fuzzy covering.

Wild Mushrooms

MORELS. The iconic fungi and a hike-stopper for any forager, the elusive morel mushroom is the most discussed and pondered of any wild food. Ron Spinosa, past president of the Minnesota Mycological Society, has an explanation: "They are probably one of the easiest of all the edible mushrooms to identify, and they are a choice edible. There are false morels that are poisonous. So you should know the difference if you plan to pick morels."

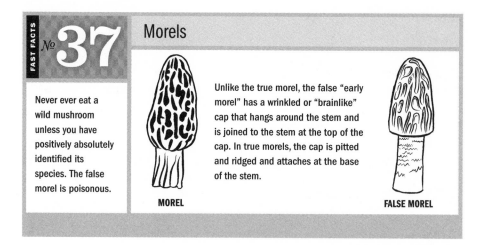

FAST FACTS № 37   Morels

Never ever eat a wild mushroom unless you have positively absolutely identified its species. The false morel is poisonous.

Unlike the true morel, the false "early morel" has a wrinkled or "brainlike" cap that hangs around the stem and is joined to the stem at the top of the cap. In true morels, the cap is pitted and ridged and attaches at the base of the stem.

MOREL

FALSE MOREL

Here are a few ways to find morels. Dead elms trees are the telltale suggestion that morels might be growing nearby, but "you might look at a hundred dead elms before you find morels," Spinosa says. One key is to look for elms with the bark sloughing off. "The elm has to be in the right stage of 'deadness,'" Spinosa adds. But don't worry if you can't find elms. Spinosa often looks around clusters of dead sumac, along railroad tracks, in old apple orchards, and along the edges of forest clearings, where elms like to grow. Morels can sometimes appear in surprising places. Spinosa said, "One of the largest morels I've ever seen was discovered by a guy in St. Paul who found it in his window well!" When to look? You can't go wrong to time your search when lilacs first start to bloom, which is early to mid-May, although in recent years they have begun to appear in mid-April. Another indicator, from the colorful lore of morel hunting, is when oak leaves are the size of squirrel's ears. "Usually by the end of May, morels are played out," Spinosa says.

FALL MUSHROOMS. "In terms of mushroom diversity, fall is the best time, because that's when you will find the most quantity and variety of mushrooms," Spinosa says. One of his favorites is the porcini, which is the Italian name for *Boletus edulis* (or *King Bolete* in America). Boletes differ from most mushrooms in that they have pores and not gills on the undersides of their caps. Another fall favorite is the sulfur shelf mushroom, also called the "chicken of the woods." The chicken of the woods is a large, bright-yellow-and-orange mushroom that grows on oak trees and stumps. It is part of a family of fungi known as polypores. The sulfur shelf is considered one of the state's best-tasting mushrooms if found in fresh, good condition. Another fall mushroom is called the "hen of the woods." The hen of the woods is a large, grayish brown polypore mushroom that grows on the ground near stumps or at the base of oak trees. A single hen of the woods can weigh twenty pounds.

MUSHROOM KNOW-HOW. Mushroom foraging should never be attempted without some education and perhaps mentoring. Never ever eat a wild mushroom unless you have positively absolutely identified its species. The Minnesota Mycological Society is good place to learn about mushrooms from experts. There are also a number of good identification books. Spinosa recommends *The Complete Mushroom Hunter* and *The National Audubon Society Field Guide to North American Mushrooms* by Gary Lincoff and *Start Mushrooming* by Stan Tekiela and Karen Shanberg.

Detasseling Corn: The Hows and Whys

CORN DETASSELING is a tradition of the Corn Belt states that typically employs teenagers for several weeks in midsummer. For kids, it is considered a hot, itchy, monotonous, and low-paying job. For their parents—many of whom detasseled corn themselves—it's a rite of passage that imbues a life lesson: manual labor is a less desirable path in life than what springs from a good education.

The act of detasseling is manually removing the top of a corn plant so it cannot pollinate itself, which it does naturally. It's the crucial step in creating a crop of hybrid corn seed. The top of the stalk, the tassel, is the male part of the corn, which produces millions of grains of pollen. The silk on the corn is the female part. When seed corn companies want to hybridize two varieties of corn, an act designed to combine the best traits of each into a superior variety, they plant the two varieties in the same field. One variety is detasseled so it will produce the new hybrid seed corn; the other type isn't detasseled and is allowed to pollinate the other.

The first act in detasseling is actually mechanical. A special machine travels through the field, cutting or pulling off tassels. Mechanical detasseling seems far more efficient than manual, but corn stalks don't grow to uniform heights, and the machine misses some tassels, so anywhere from 10 to 40 percent of the tassels need to be removed.

After the machine is done, corn detasselers take to the field, walking down the rows, breaking off the remaining tassels on the five- to eight-foot-tall stalks and dropping them on the ground. The tools of the trade are simple: a pair of gloves, a hat, sunscreen, a pair of comfortable tennis shoes for walking, and maybe an iPod loaded with your favorite tunes to relieve the boredom. Work often begins at dawn, when dew lies heavily on corn plants, so workers wear rain jackets, rain ponchos, or plastic garbage bags to fend off the moisture in the morning.

Companies typically provide workers with gloves, a hat with face netting to shield from pollen and insects, and a pair of safety glasses. Workers are paid hourly—anywhere from minimum wage to twelve dollars an hour if you're experienced—or by the row. A day might begin cool and chilly, with dew providing an extra soaking, and by the afternoon, it is stifling hot and humid.

Farmers are picky about getting every tassel because any remaining is money out of the farmer's pocket. A few remaining stalks with tassels can ruin a field. To ensure that nearly all the tassels are gone, two to three passes are made through each field.

One recent estimate published in the *Wall Street Journal* put the number of teen-age detasselers working each season at one hundred thousand. Seed corn companies will hire detasseling crews, put them on school buses, and take them to fields. Detasselers talk about the hard work but also of the esprit de corps of the job and surviving the ordeal together.

But manual detasseling could become a thing of the past. Seed corn companies are developing male-sterile corn, which means it doesn't produce tassels and pollen. That would put detasselers out of business.

Ice Sculpting at the Winter Carnival

Larry Fischer stood before an admiring audience. A big man, Fischer looked like he could easily heft a hundred-pound block of ice, but today he was dressed for the indoors, in black slacks and dress shirt. The audience inside the Central Library in St. Paul wanted to learn how Fischer turned ice blocks into fanciful swans, Viking ships, and improbable spheres with graceful, curving supports.

The St. Paul Winter Carnival was in full swing, and outside the library, the hum of chainsaws, die grinders, and rotary sanders denoted competitive ice carvers hard at work. Fischer was inside, not competing in this year's carnival, but ready to share his secrets.

"I just love the medium of ice," says the culinary arts teacher, who serves as the carnival's master carver for special events and who first won the individual carving competition in 1985. "You can't make any money at it, but you can compete all over the world—China, Japan, Alaska."

His introduction. Fischer, who teaches ice sculpting at St. Paul College, became interested in the art form in the early 1970s. As a high school student, he tried sculpting in wood and clay, but he later chose a career in the culinary arts and began working at a variety of big-name restaurants in the Twin Cities. (He currently teaches cake and pastry skills at St. Paul College.) He began carving fruits such as pineapples and watermelons for catering displays, and he attempted his first ice carving while a chef student. He later decided to try a large ice sculpture while working at the Minnesota Club. The bird was a hit, and Fischer was inspired to enter the Winter Carnival competition, which at the time was limited to individual carvers and not teams. In the first few years, he placed no higher than fourth. In 1985, he won. "It was a big ego boost," he says. He went on to win the individual competition five more times. In the individual category, artists have two ten-by-twenty-by-forty-inch blocks of ice and five hours to carve their works.

Fischer was part of the team that built the sprawling, to-scale replica of the Minnesota Capitol in Rice Park during the 2005 Winter Carnival, considered one of the hallmark sculptures of the carnival. His teams have won four first place awards over the years.

TEAM COMPETITION. Fischer's forte is carving large, multiblock pieces. At the Winter Carnival, it's called the team multiblock competition, in which each team gets twenty blocks of ice, sized at forty by twenty by ten inches and weighing about three hundred pounds. Each team has forty-eight hours to craft the blocks into an awe-inspiring work. Each work takes meticulous planning and, of course, teamwork to organize, cut, and lift the blocks into place. The sculptures are judged on their creativity and originality, technical difficulty, use of ice, three-dimensional qualities, and detail.

In 2003, Fischer and his team built the giant sphere and a Viking ship in forty hours, an exhausting effort that required Fischer to carve for thirty-six hours straight. The sphere took second place, the Viking ship third. The ship also earned the People's Choice Award. Winning the team competition nets each team two thousand dollars. "I'm never disappointed in my work, whether I win or lose," Fischer says. "It's a joy being around the other carvers and in the park, although the cash is nice to use to buy a few new power tools."

HOW HE STARTS. Fischer says he is sure there are lots of mathematical equations and engineering concepts he could apply to ice carving, especially the larger pieces, but he isn't that technical when tackling a new project. He starts with pictures of an object and then begins drawing it on graph paper. After he sketches the piece, he

Sphere by Larry Fischer, Rob Graham, and Tom Schiller

builds a scale model, usually out of foam. His scale is one inch to every ten inches of the project. With some projects, he cuts cardboard templates of each ice piece in his basement and uses them to make sure every block is cut to specifications. "I'm not a great carver, but a pretty good designer," he says. "Competitions aren't won in the park but back on the desk before the competition." Some planning for his sculptures begins way back in November, Fischer says.

TEACHING BEGINNERS. In his ice-sculpting classes, Fischer has students find three-dimensional drawings of the chosen subject, such as an eagle or grizzly bear. After they study pictures of the figure, he turns students loose with paring knives on bars of Ivory soap, a perfect medium in which to practice, he says. "It takes the fear out of carving because no one is scared of making a mistake with a bar of soap." While the soap is far from replicating the hard and brittle nature of ice, it can crack and flake if not carved with care. Soap is also cheap, "cheaper than a huge block of ice that can cost forty dollars," Fischer says.

TOOLS. An ice carver's toolbox contains many of the same tools a carpenter uses: coping saws (small, fine-toothed saws for cutting curves and corners), chisels, die grinders (with rotating and cutting tips), sanders, drills, and small electric chainsaws (and a few gas-powered ones for bigger cuts). Tool manufacturers have tapped into the ice sculpting (and wood sculpting) world, designing specialty power tools and saws that make precision cuts easier and faster. Fischer says that by far the most important tools for sculptors are chainsaws, which are available with specialty small-sized bars and chains for delicate cutting. Chainsaw tips are now made the diameter of quarters and dimes. He says chainsaws for ice don't require special oil lubricants that are used for cutting wood, but sculptors still need to clean and apply anti-rusting lubricants.

THE PERFECT CONDITIONS. Above-freezing temperatures obviously pose a challenge for ice sculptors, but other weather conditions can be tricky, too. Sunny days aren't good, Fischer says, because the heat of the sun can melt sculptures just like warm temperatures. Wind is a curse, too. "A warm wind just eats it up, especially if it's above freezing," Fischer explains. His ideal sculpting days are overcast and about twenty degrees above zero.

DELICATE CUTS. Ice sculptors are incorporating more and more delicate detail into their works, including strands of flowing hair and thin, tubelike elements, such as an arrow in a bow held by an archer. There is a technique to creating long and thin vertical details using freezing water poured over string, but other delicate features rely heavily on the skills of the sculptor. Break off the delicate piece, and it can be "welded" back to the sculpture, but there will be an undesirable seam at the break. "It doesn't take much to break some of these thin strands," Fischer says. "To cut them, you have to have the ideal conditions."

AN AFTERNOON AT THE WINTER CARNIVAL. It is late afternoon when Fischer completes his lecture, and the crowd ventures back outside to Rice Park, where the Sunday throngs are thinning but not by much. The park is a museum of large icy lions, polar bears, totem poles, unicorns, and a Pegasus. A block of ice has been transformed into a ballerina in the time it took Fischer to describe his talents and techniques. A crowd gathers around a large, otherworldly sculpture that depicts elfish creatures operating a machine that makes plate-sized snowflakes and winter shapes. The sculpture, called *Das Wintermachenmachine*, a kind of Dr. Seuss winter-making machine created by Rob Graham, Terry Reis, and Tom Schiller, ends up winning the multiblock competition and the two-thousand-dollar prize.

"This is just *so* cool," explains a woman, gazing at the imaginative sculpture. It is twenty-two degrees, a perfect day for making ice sculptures—and admiring the imagination and skill of their creators.

Become a Phenologist

PHENOLOGY IS A BRANCH of science that studies the cycles of plants and animals and their relationships with climate. Anyone who records the arrival of the first bluebird in spring or the dropping of white oak acorns in the fall or the flowering of water lilies in the summer is a phenologist. Backyard bird-watchers, deer hunters, and blueberry pickers use their phenological observations to track the birds, deer, and berries they're so keenly interested in.

Larry Weber, a retired schoolteacher in Wrenshall, Minnesota, has been a phenologist for nearly forty years. He began keeping a daily nature journal on January

1, 1975. He hasn't missed a day since, writing at least several pages of observations daily. He taught a phenology-based science class for twenty-five years.

"Phenology is often concerned with the first happenings, but I believe that phenology is not 'first-ology,' and I watch the entire season changing—the first, last, peak, flowering, fruiting, growing of leaves, and dropping leaves," he says. "I started just because I think that nature is so amazing to watch and I find that these records make me take a closer look and become aware of the phenomena around us."

His phenology records began with noting the springtime return of birds and when flowers bloomed, but before long his recordkeeping started to include mammals, amphibians (especially frogs), reptiles, insects such as butterflies, dragonflies, and spiders, wildflowers, trees, and even fungi. He also watches the weather very carefully.

"It is not necessary to go as into phenology as I do, but it is a great way to get to know more about the nature around us," he says. "At a time when so many people have so little interest in nature, phenology is a great way to open more interest."

Another avid Minnesota phenologist was the late waterfowl research pioneer Art Hawkins, who kept a journal of nature and weather in his backyard starting in 1957. When I interviewed the Lino Lakes retired scientist in 1996, when he was eighty-three, Hawkins had filled nearly forty volumes of his nature journals. When he died in 2006 at age ninety-two, Hawkins was one of the oldest living students of Aldo Leopold, the father of modern wildlife management and another famous phenologist.

Phenology is part of Minnesota's mainstream media. The *Duluth News Tribune* runs a column every spring called *Spring Watch*, where readers e-mail or call in their observations about the arrival of spring. The public radio station in Grand Rapids, KAXE, has a "staff phenologist" in John Latimer, a rural mail carrier who has been making nature and climate observations on the radio since 1983. The popular Minnesota Weatherguide Environment Calendar has a special phenology section written by well-known naturalist Jim Gilbert.

As Weber suggests, it's easy to be a phenologist. You can do it from your kitchen or living room window. Start by keeping a notebook or calendar in which you can record your daily observations of nature. It helps if your window looks out into the woods, some prairie grass, or a lake, or if you have a birdfeeder. Phenology isn't much fun if you're watching a city street or gas station. Record the seasonal arrivals and departures of songbird species. Note the ice-in and ice-out dates on your lake or neighborhood pond. Record when the last leaves fall off your maple tree in the fall or when your crocuses pop out of the ground. By returning to your nature calendar or notebook each year, you can compare seasonal trends and predict natural events.

For today's phenologists, electronic weather stations, which record daily highs and lows, humidity, and sometimes barometric pressure, are especially handy for recording daily climate changes.

Building a canoe for Mille Lacs Trading Post, 1940

Appendix

Skill-Building Resources

THE NORTH HOUSE FOLK SCHOOL, located on Lake Superior's North Shore in Grand Marais, was inspired by a folk school concept that originated in Denmark in the mid-1800s. The idea is to teach traditional arts and crafts in a hands-on, non-competitive classroom. North House was started in the mid-1990s by Grand Marais citizens and volunteers; a board of directors was founded in January 1997. Today the school offers dozens of classes ranging from boatbuilding and timber framing to knitting and fiber arts, traditional cooking arts, and food preservation. Classes are affordable, and the school's setting, overlooking the Grand Marais harbor, is inspiring. The school is located 275 miles from the Twin Cities at the intersection of Minnesota 61 and Fifth Avenue West in Grand Marais. The website is www.northhouse.org. Phone: 888-387-9762.

University of Minnesota Extension is a font of information on farming, gardening, food preservation, and many other life-enhancing skills. The Extension oversees the state's Master Gardener program, which provides online and in-person advice on successful gardening. The Extension has good online resources on home food safety and food preservation. For information, go to www.extension.umn.edu.

The Minnesota Department of Natural Resources offers a number of skills-building classes for outdoors people. It oversees the state's safety-training programs for firearms, bow hunting, boating, all-terrain vehicle riding, and snowmobiling. The classes are taught by certified volunteer instructors. The agency also directs the Becoming an Outdoors Woman (BOW) skills-building classes for women; MinnAqua, a fishing and aquatic education program; and, in the spring, free maple syrup making classes at state parks. The agency has recently embarked on a series of "I Can" classes that teach camping, paddling, fishing, and rock climbing at state parks. For more information, go to www.mndnr.gov or call 651-296-6157 or 888-646-6367.

In many ways, skill building for children is more accessible than for adults. Youth summer camps are an excellent opportunity to learn all manner of skills, whether it's canoeing, camping, water sports, arts and languages, or computer-skills building. Boy Scouts and Girl Scouts are still a gold standard for outdoors, leadership, and social-skill building. The Minnesota 4-H, operated by the University of Minnesota Extension, remains a vital skill-building program for rural, urban, and suburban youngsters. Minnesota's environmental learning centers are scattered around the state and offer youth and adult programming about nature and outdoors skills. The Science Museum of Minnesota is another source for youth science and outdoor skill learning.

Recommended Reading

Edwin Tappan Adney and Howard I. Chapelle, *The Bark Canoes and Skin Boats of North America* (New York: Skyhorse Publishing, 2007).

Ball Blue Book of Preserving (Alltrista Consumer Products, 2004).

Garrett Conover and Alexandra Conover, *The Winter Wilderness Companion* (Camden, ME: Ragged Mountain Press, 2001).

Carrol Henderson, *Woodworking for Wildlife* and *Landscaping for Wildlife* (St. Paul: Minnesota Department of Natural Resources, 1992, 1987).

Cliff Jacobson, *Boundary Waters Canoe Camping* (Guilford, CT: Globe Pequot Press, 2000).

Gary Lincoff, *The National Audubon Society Field Guide to North American Mushrooms* (New York: Knopf, 1981).

Bill Mason, *The Path of the Paddle* (Richmond Hill, ON: Firefly Books, 1999).

Gary and Joanie McGuffin, *Paddle Your Own Canoe* (Richmond Hill, ON: Boston Mills Press, 2003).

Daniel Pauly, *Exploring the Boundary Waters* (Minneapolis: University of Minnesota Press, 2005).

Susan Mahnke Peery and Charles G. Reavis, *Home Sausage Making* (North Adams, MA: Storey Publishing, 2003).

Frank Philbrick and Stephen Philbrick, *The Backyard Lumberjack* (North Adams, MA: Storey Publishing, 2006).

David Allan Sibley, *The Sibley Guide to Birds* (New York: Knopf, 2000).

Welby R. Smith, *Trees and Shrubs of Minnesota* (Minneapolis: University of Minnesota Press, 2008).

Mark Sparky Stensaas, *Rock Picker's Guide to Lake Superior's North Shore* (Duluth, MN: Kollath-Stensaas Publishing, 2000).

Stan Tekiela and Karen Shanberg, *Start Mushrooming* (Cambridge, MN: Adventure Publications, 1993).

Linda Ziedrich, *The Joy of Pickling* (Boston: Harvard Common Press, 2009).

Index

Italicized page numbers indicate a photo

Image Credits

Sketches by Mason Sklar

pages ii, viii, xii, 194
                Shutterstock

pages 11, 12   supplied by Alan Burchell

pages 24, 26, 49, 54, 65, 109, 130, 136, 156, 157
                supplied by the author

page 81   supplied by Erik Simula

page 96   stamp image property of the United States Fish and Wildlife Service

page 100   supplied by Liz Schreiber

page 104   supplied by Dave Freeman

page 132   supplied by Marty Hanson

page 151   photo by John Brandauer

page 185   supplied by Larry Fischer

All other photographs from Minnesota Historical Society collections

Designed and typeset by Diana Boger.

Display fonts include venerable Clarendon, melodramatic Isabella, quirky Runic, and Franklin Gothic Condensed. Body type is Miller Text, a Scotch Roman font popular in the early nineteenth century.